The Natural History of Eastern Massachusetts

Written by Stan Freeman
Illustrated by Mike Nasuti

Eastern chipmunk

Monarch

Wild columbine

Ring-necked pheasant

Hampshire House Publishing Co.
Florence, Mass.

The Natural History of Eastern Massachusetts

Published by: Hampshire House Publishing Co.
8 Nonotuck St.
Florence, Mass. 01062

First printing
Copyright © 1998 by Stan Freeman
and Mike Nasuti

Photo editors: Domingo "Dino" Diaz
and Stan Freeman
Copy editors: Karin Henry, Austin
Kenefick, Irmina Pulc and Barry Schatz
Additional illustrations: Donna Blazey

ISBN: 0-9636814-3-5
Library of Congress catalogue card number: 98-71823
Printed on recycled paper in the USA

Some of the material in this book is based on articles by the authors that originally appeared in the

**Springfield Union-News
and the
Sunday Republican**

The authors would like to thank the following people and organizations for their advice and help in preparing and reviewing the material in this book: Tom Tyning, Massachusetts Audubon Society; Bill Davis and the staff of the Massachusetts Division of Fisheries and Wildlife; Michael Williams, David Bloniarz, Jeff Boettner, Alan Richmond, Scott Jackson, Adam Porter – University of Massachusetts; Mary Lou Curran, Peabody Essex Museum; Barbara Pryor, New England Wild Flower Society; Greg Sawyer, Massachusetts Division of Marine Fisheries; Jim Notchey, National Weather Service; Curt Osgood, Westover Air Reserve Base Weather Station; and Dale Ruff and the staff photographers of the Springfield Union-News.

This series highlights the natural history of individual states or regions of states. Many species of wildlife, such as American robins and oxeye daisies, can be found throughout the United States. And some subjects, such as the metamorphosis of tadpoles into frogs and the formation of lightning, apply equally to all states. So some information in this book, including text, illustrations and photographs, is repeated from book to book in the series.

Cape Cod National Seashore

Contents

Bumble bee

Black bear

Sugar maple leaf

Contents

Northern cardinal

Garter snake

White-tailed deer

Geology

Once in the region now called New England, there were mountains that may have soared as high as Mount Everest. Once there were fiery volcanoes and, at other times, mile-high glaciers. Once what are now Boston and the coast of Maine lay on another continent separated from North America by a vast ocean.

Hard to believe? Not for geologists, for whom a million years is the mere blink of an eye. They know that right now is a quiet time in the geologic cycle, a momentary calm amid the violent upheavals that have marked the history of the region's landscape.

For a glimpse of what New England may have looked like in other times, one needs only to travel to the western United States. At several points in its history, New England looked very much like the landscape from Colorado to California, with mountains more towering than the Rockies.

The earth's crust, or surface layer, is made up of vast rock plates, with an average thickness of about 60 miles, which form the continents and the ocean floor. There are about 20 of these plates covering the earth's surface, arranged like pieces in a jigsaw puzzle. Essentially, they "float" on a layer of denser rock found deeper in the earth, pushed along by the currents of heat rising up from inside the earth. The earth's core has a temperature of more than 8,000 degrees Fahrenheit (°F).

The continental plates are always in motion, coming together and drawing apart, perhaps moving a few inches a year. This is called continental drift.

Even at this slow speed, though, when these massive plates push against each other, geologic fireworks happen – mountains gradually rise into the air, volcanoes may erupt and earthquakes might rumble.

That's what's happening currently in the western United States. The Pacific and North American plates are slowly sliding by each other, grinding together along their edges. About 65 million years ago, when the plates were pushing right into each other, this process was creating the Rocky Mountains, which are considered "young" mountains. (Scientists believe the earth is about 4.6 billion years old.)

New England is also part of the North American plate, but for nearly 190 million years, this plate has been moving away from the plate that is next to it on the east, the one on which Africa is located. So there are no strong geologic pressures on New England's part of the plate to create or enlarge mountains. As a result, the magnificent mountains that were formed in the region during the last collision of continental plates 280 million years ago have spent those millions of years being slowly eroded by the weather.

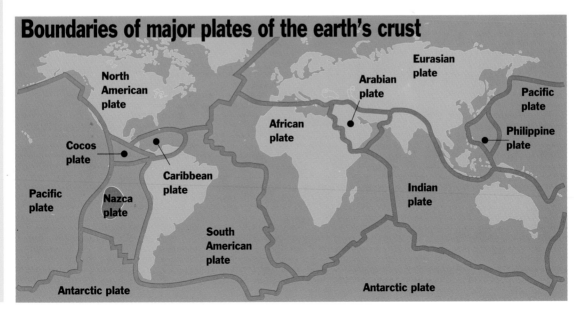

Boundaries of major plates of the earth's crust

North American plate

Eurasian plate

Arabian plate

Pacific plate

African plate

Philippine plate

Cocos plate

Caribbean plate

Indian plate

Pacific plate

Nazca plate

South American plate

Antarctic plate

Antarctic plate

The rock cycle

Rocks have their own life cycle, and it begins on the surface of the earth with sand, pebbles, shells and other debris that become cemented together over the course of time. The rocks they form are called sedimentary rocks, one of three categories of rocks along with metamorphic and igneous.

Eventually, sedimentary rocks, such as sandstone and shale, are buried by layers of other sedimentary rocks. With the heat and pressure deeper inside the earth, they can become harder, turning to metamorphic rocks such as quartzite, schist and gneiss.

Metamorphic rocks may eventually move to the surface as the result of earthquakes or the erosion of the land above them.

But if metamorphic rocks move deeper into the earth, the higher temperatures there can turn them to molten rock. If this molten material hardens underground it can become igneous rock such as granite. If it surges up to the earth's surface through a volcano as lava and hardens, it will become another form of igneous rock such as basalt.

Harsh weather and the freezing and thawing through the seasons will eventually chip away at surface rocks. These chips may then become part of new sedimentary rocks, continuing the cycle.

Sandstone – *Sedimentary; formed from sand*

Granite – *Igneous; formed when molten rock cools underground*

Slate – *Metamorphic; formed from shale at low temperatures*

Conglomerate – *Sedimentary; formed from mix of sand and gravel*

Shale – *Sedimentary; formed from mud and clay*

Gneiss – *Metamorphic; formed from igneous and sedimentary rocks*

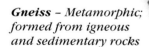

Schist – *Metamorphic; often formed from shale*

Rock or mineral?

● Minerals, such as diamond or quartz, are usually made up of only a few chemical elements, and they have crystalline structures. Rocks, such as conglomerate or granite, may be made up of combinations of minerals and bits of other rocks. While elements of a rock may have crystalline structures, the overall rock usually does not.

Quartz, a mineral

Drifting continents

Three times in the last 500 million years, the east coast of North America has collided with other continental plates. These collisions did much to shape Massachusetts, adding land to the state in each instance. Although continental plates may move only inches a year, their masses are so great that once they come together they may continue to push against each other for millions of years, creating mountains, earthquakes and volcanoes in the region of the collision.

The theory of continental drift became widely accepted by scientists only in the 1960s. So the positions and shapes of the continents through geologic history are still being estimated.

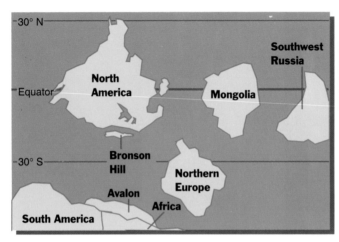

500 million years ago

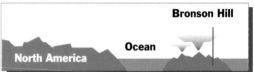

The land that will be Massachusetts is scattered south of the equator on various continents. Trees, plants and animals have not yet appeared on land. Primitive life is developing in the oceans. Approaching North America from the south is a plate covered with volcanoes, called Bronson Hill by geologists, that is about to collide with the coast.

455 million years ago

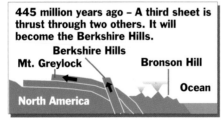

455 million years ago – Bronson Hill collides with North America forcing sheets of rock up onto the continent.

445 million years ago – A third sheet is thrust through two others. It will become the Berkshire Hills.

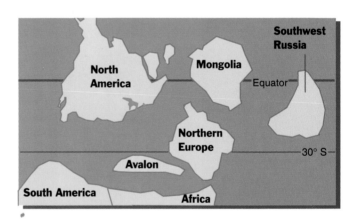

Bronson Hill collides with the North American coast, pushing up layers of rock, one of which will become the Berkshire Hills. To the west of the Berkshires, the collision pushes up the Taconic Mountains, including Mount Greylock. Avalon, another plate, has broken free of the united African-South American continent and is drifting north. It contains land that will eventually become Boston.

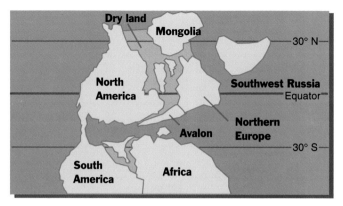

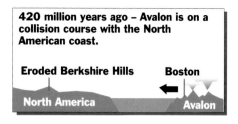

420 million years ago

420 million years ago – Avalon is on a collision course with the North American coast.

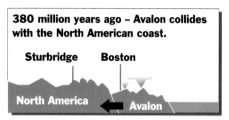

380 million years ago – Avalon collides with the North American coast.

Avalon collides with North America, folding up layers of land like an accordion. Huge mountain ranges form in Central Massachusetts. Past Avalon, out in the ocean, a third plate is approaching, the African continent. North America is slowly drifting north but is still largely south of the equator. Primitive fish fill the seas, and plants are starting to flourish on land.

280 million years ago

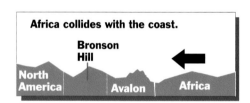

Africa collides with the coast.

Africa collides with North America. More debris is heaped on Massachusetts, which now lies near the equator. There is also more folding of the land, forming mountains. All seven continents are now joined in a single vast continent, called Pangaea by geologists. Dinosaurs will soon appear.

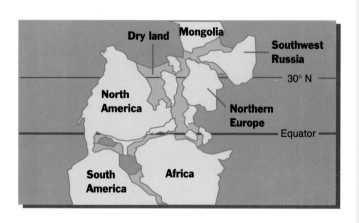

190 million years ago

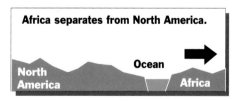

Africa separates from North America.

Africa begins to separate from North America, causing fractures of the land. The gap that finally forms between the separating continents is the start of the Atlantic Ocean. Dinosaurs now dominate the earth, but the earliest human beings will not appear for another 188 million years.

The bedrock of Eastern Massachusetts

If you dig down beneath the loose dirt and rocks on the earth's surface, you will eventually strike bedrock, solid rock that is often the same type of rock for miles around. In coastal areas or on steep mountain slopes, you may not have to dig deeply at all to find bedrock. In river valleys, where flooding has deposited layer upon layer of silt and clay over the centuries, you may have to dig down a hundred feet or more.

The land masses that came together to form Eastern Massachusetts over millions of years carried different kinds and ages of bedrock with them. Like different colors of modeling clay pushed together, the bedrock beneath the region is divided into zones of those different types of rock.

In much of Worcester County, you will find metamorphic bedrock, such as schist and gneiss, that was once part of another continent, perhaps South America.

Closer to the coast, around Boston and in southeastern Massachusetts, you will also find metamorphic bedrock, but it is rock that was once part of Africa.

Southwest of Boston, in parts of Norfolk, Plymouth and Bristol counties, you will also find sedimentary bedrock, such as sandstone and conglomerate, that was gradually laid down over older metamorphic bedrock.

About 280 million years ago, some of the Eastern Massachusetts bedrock was broken up in places by the collision of the African continental plate with the North American plate. Molten rock from deeper in the earth was injected into the cracks in the bedrock. It cooled and hardened to become igneous rock, mainly granite.

On top of the bedrock of Cape Cod, Nantucket and Martha's Vineyard lies a layer of rocks, gravel, sand and other material dropped there about 18,500 years ago by a melting glacier as the last ice age ended.

These piles of glacial debris are the reason Cape Cod and the Massachusetts islands sit above the surface of the ocean.

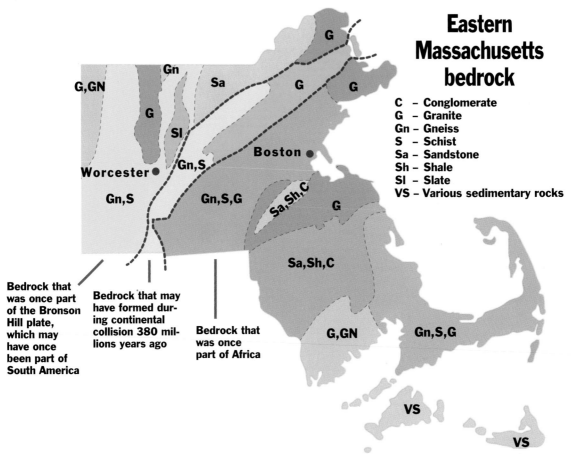

Eastern Massachusetts bedrock

C – Conglomerate
G – Granite
Gn – Gneiss
S – Schist
Sa – Sandstone
Sh – Shale
Sl – Slate
VS – Various sedimentary rocks

Bedrock that was once part of the Bronson Hill plate, which may have once been part of South America

Bedrock that may have formed during continental collision 380 millions years ago

Bedrock that was once part of Africa

Earthquakes

New England. Land of maple syrup, autumn foliage and earthquakes.

Earthquakes?

In fact, two or three times each month earthquakes do rumble through the New England countryside.

While earthquake sensors in the region record these events, most people don't even notice them. A few dishes and window panes may rattle. A few startled house cats may stop in their tracks. But for the most part, they are small quakes that can easily be mistaken for an overloaded truck passing nearby.

That is not to say that a large quake could not hit New England. In 1755, an earthquake rocked Cape Ann, knocking the weather vane off Faneuil Hall in Boston more than 30 miles to the south. The Boston County Journal that year reported the event this way:

"The visible effects of the earthquake are considerable in the town [Boston] ... Many chimneys, I conjecture from my observation, not much less than 100, are levell'd with the roofs of the houses. Not fewer than 12 of 1500 are shattered and thrown down in part. So that in some places ... the streets are almost covered with the bricks that have fallen."

While the Cape Ann quake may have been powerful by New England standards, it was small in comparison to quakes that have rocked other parts of the world. The San Francisco earthquake of 1906, perhaps the strongest quake in the continental United States in modern times, is believed to have been about 100 times as powerful as the Cape Ann quake.

Most earthquakes occur in places in the world where the continental plates come together, areas called faults. As two adjoining plates move in relation to each other, the rocky edges on each side of the fault line can grab hold, locking the plates together. Gradually, pressure builds up as the plates continue to move while the area around the faults does not, like pressure building up in a spring that is stretched. Finally, the rock on one side or the other of the fault line suddenly breaks. And this causes a violent shifting of the plates around the fault line, sending out shock waves in all directions that are felt as an earthquake.

New England is in the middle of the North American continental plate. But there are ancient faults – partial breaks and tears in the plate – in the region. And it is stress along these faults that causes the region's many minor quakes.

Earth's history

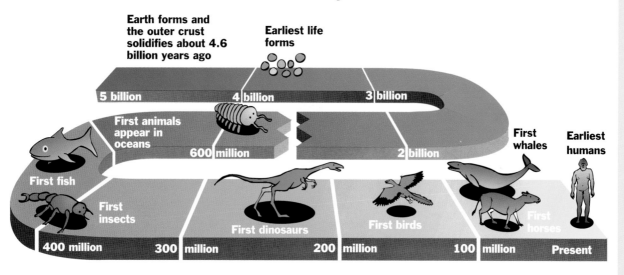

Earth forms and the outer crust solidifies about 4.6 billion years ago

Earliest life forms

5 billion   4 billion   3 billion

First animals appear in oceans

600 million   2 billion

First whales

Earliest humans

First fish

First insects

First dinosaurs

First birds

First horses

400 million   300 million   200 million   100 million   Present

Dinosaurs

The terrible lizard: translated from Greek, that's what *dinosaur* actually means. For nearly 165 million years, from about 230 million years ago to 65 million years ago, these legendary beasts roamed just about everywhere on earth, including New England.

Wherever you walk in the region, the fierce tyrannosaurus rex and the massive triceratops once walked. But while scientists find the bones of these ancient creatures in other regions, they do not find them in New England.

For bones to survive and fossilize, or turn to rock, they must be buried by sand or mud very quickly. Bones left out on the surface will scatter and decay. And when they are buried, if the water in the ground is too acidic or the soil is too rich in oxygen, the bones will also deteriorate before they turn to fossils. New England has both acidic ground water and oxygen-rich soil.

What geologists do find in New England are fossilized footprints of dinosaurs. In fact, the Connecticut River Valley in Western Massachusetts is considered one of the richest places on earth in which to find dinosaur tracks embedded in rock.

A rock bearing the imprint of dinosaurs is like a photograph that is millions of years old. It's a snapshot in stone of events of perhaps one warm summer morning by the shores of an ancient river or lake. A dinosaur might have wandered down to the edge of the water to drink, pressing its feet into the soft mud created by a rainstorm the evening before. In the hot sun, the mud and prints dried and hardened and were buried by other layers of mud containing still more dinosaur prints.

Coelophysis

Over the centuries, the buried layers and prints would turn to rock such as shale. Erosion and earthquakes eventually brought some of the print-bearing rocks back to the surface, allowing a geologist to crack apart the layers to reveal the tracks, like someone turning the pages of a photo album.

Even though they are millions of years old, the footprints the rocks contain can show great detail. Sometimes, the texture of the skin on the bottom of a dinosaur's foot is so clear in the print that the scales can actually be counted.

From about 220 to 190 million years ago, conditions in the newly formed (in geologic terms) Connecticut River Valley

The Mesozoic era – the age of dinosaurs 230 – 65 million years ago

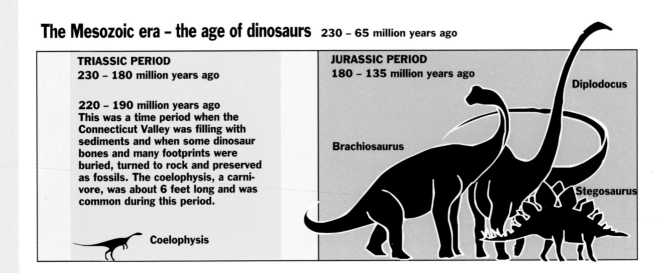

TRIASSIC PERIOD
230 – 180 million years ago

220 – 190 million years ago
This was a time period when the Connecticut Valley was filling with sediments and when some dinosaur bones and many footprints were buried, turned to rock and preserved as fossils. The coelophysis, a carnivore, was about 6 feet long and was common during this period.

Coelophysis

JURASSIC PERIOD
180 – 135 million years ago

Diplodocus

Brachiosaurus

Stegosaurus

How dinosaur footprints were formed

The Connecticut River Valley about 200 million years ago

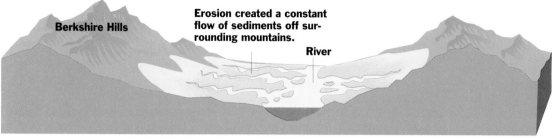

Berkshire Hills

Erosion created a constant flow of sediments off surrounding mountains.

River

1. Tracks left by a dinosaur in soft mud after a rainstorm might dry and harden in the hot sun over the course of several days.

2. Another rainstorm might wash a new layer of mud over the footprints, filling them in. Then this layer might fill with new tracks, which might also harden in the sun.

3. Over the course of time, layer would build upon layer, and the original set of tracks might be hundreds of feet underground, where the hardened mud would eventually turn to rock under the intense pressure.

were just right for creating fossilized tracks. The sides of the valley were very steep, and after rainstorms mud would flow down the slopes into the flat areas where rivers and lakes could be found.

However, that era was in the early part of the age of

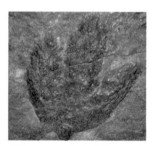

Dinosaur print in rock

dinosaurs, before the larger and better known of their breed, such as the stegosaurus and brontosaurus, had developed. So the largest of the footprints that have been found in the Connecticut River Valley may be from animals that were about the size of elephants.

Cenozoic era 65 million years ago – present

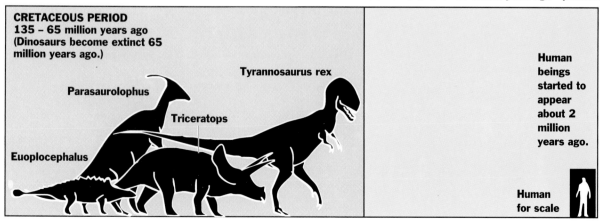

CRETACEOUS PERIOD
135 – 65 million years ago
(Dinosaurs become extinct 65 million years ago.)

Parasaurolophus

Triceratops

Tyrannosaurus rex

Euoplocephalus

Human beings started to appear about 2 million years ago.

Human for scale

Ice age

It was the dead of winter even in the heart of summer. It was the ice age, and during the last two million years, there have been as many as 20 ice ages in North America.

The most recent ice age began about 28,000 years ago when a glacier formed in eastern Canada and slowly expanded, eventually covering most of the Northeast. In some places, the ice was more than a mile thick. The glacier, called by geologists the Laurentide ice sheet, also spread west, covering most of Canada and the northernmost United States from the Rocky Mountains eastward. It did not begin to melt away from the Northeast until about 18,500 years ago.

Glaciers form when the climate cools enough so that snow builds up in winter faster than it melts in summer. Just as a snowball turns to an ice ball if you squeeze it hard enough, a pile of snow, if it continues to grow, can eventually become so compressed that much of it turns to ice, especially at the bottom. The increase in snow and ice year in and year out can create a mound of ice so high that the weight of it causes the ice to begin to flow outward at the bottom, like thick maple syrup flowing on a tabletop, except at a much slower pace. A glacier may advance at a speed of only a few feet a year.

Even at this slow speed, though, a glacier can travel a great distance over thousands of years, as it did during the last ice age.

Like clay in the hands of a sculptor, Eastern Massachusetts took much of its shape from the last glacier that reached down into New England. If there had been no glacier, there would be no Cape Cod, Martha's Vineyard or Nantucket today.

A glacier can be like a vacuum cleaner, drawing up into the ice the rocks and boulders that it finds lying on the ground or digs out of the bedrock as it advances. When at last the climate warms enough so that a glacier begins to melt back, all the debris trapped in the ice is dropped to the ground, and that is why much of Massachusetts has so many loose rocks and boulders on its surface. When one of these rocks differs from the bedrock on which it has come to rest, it is called an erratic.

A glacier can also be like a bulldozer, pushing rocks and boulders along in front of it. And when it begins to melt, all that debris is left at its front edge in a long pile called a moraine. As a glacier melts back, it may pause in places, creating new moraines.

The glacier might eventually come to a location where the air is warm enough for the ice to start melting. But to the north, water will still freeze, so the glacier continues to flow forward, carrying rocks and boulders like a conveyor belt to the front edge where the ice is melting and the debris is dropping, which adds to the moraine.

When glacial ice is melting, a constant

North America's last glacier (about 18,500 years ago)

Cordilleran ice sheet

CANADA

Laurentide ice sheet

UNITED STATES

stream of water is flowing out from the glacier, usually toward the south. Boulders and large rocks tend to stay where they are once they are free of the ice. But the ice is also filled with small rocks, dirt, sand and gravel, and all this lighter debris is carried out by the flowing water. As this small debris settles to the ground, it creates what geologists call an outwash plain.

The last glacier to enter New England stopped and began to melt back when it reached Southeastern Massachusetts. So Cape Cod, the islands and Plymouth County owe much of their land to the glacial moraines and outwash plains of the region's last glacier. The soil in these areas is filled with sand, gravel and small rocks.

The region's last glacier did not completely melt away from Massachusetts until about 15,000 years ago. However, once the ice was gone from an area, the landscape did not immediately spring back to life. It was probably frozen, barren and blanketed with snow much of the year, a wasteland covered with boulders, smaller rocks, sand and other glacial debris. Woolly mammoths and mastodons roamed the land, and low tundra vegetation, similar to what you would see near the Arctic today, probably grew on it.

The first human beings arriving in the Northeast after the last ice age may have encountered very cold conditions indeed.

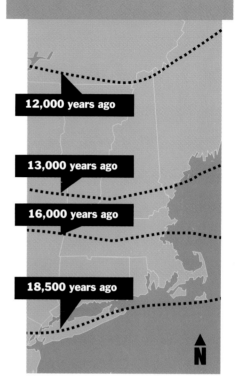

The retreating ice

By 18,500 years ago, the most recent glacier to cover New England had reached its southernmost limit and begun to melt back. By 12,000 years ago, it had retreated into Canada.

12,000 years ago

13,000 years ago

16,000 years ago

18,500 years ago

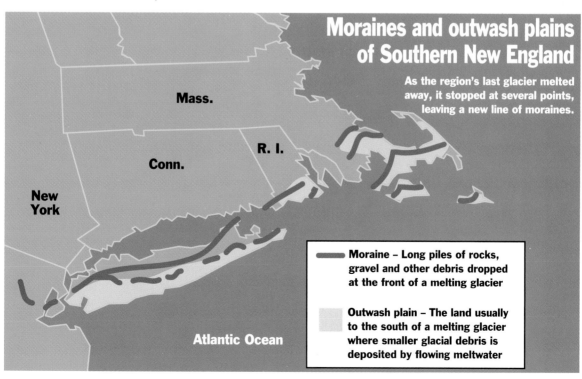

Moraines and outwash plains of Southern New England

As the region's last glacier melted away, it stopped at several points, leaving a new line of moraines.

Mass.
R. I.
Conn.
New York
Atlantic Ocean

Moraine – Long piles of rocks, gravel and other debris dropped at the front of a melting glacier

Outwash plain – The land usually to the south of a melting glacier where smaller glacial debris is deposited by flowing meltwater

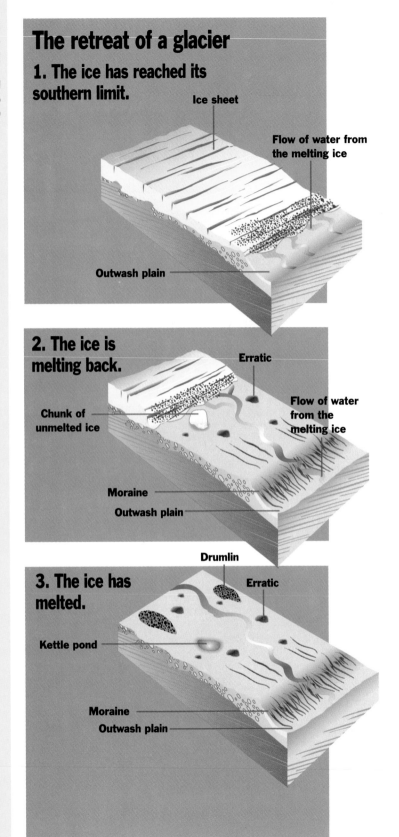

The retreat of a glacier

1. The ice has reached its southern limit.

Ice sheet

Flow of water from the melting ice

Outwash plain

2. The ice is melting back.

Erratic

Chunk of unmelted ice

Flow of water from the melting ice

Moraine

Outwash plain

3. The ice has melted.

Drumlin

Erratic

Kettle pond

Moraine

Outwash plain

Erratics

As a glacier moves over the land, it may dig out rocks and boulders from the underlying bedrock and carry them for great distances in the bottom layers of ice. When the glacier finally melts, these boulders may fall to the ground miles from where they began and miles from any bedrock of the same kind. Geologists call such boulders erratics.

Plymouth Rock, where the Pilgrims are supposed to have stepped from their ship, the Mayflower, in 1620, is perhaps the nation's most famous erratic.

Drumlins

Beneath a glacier, gravel, clay and other material can build up in places. When the glacier melts away, these piles can appear as smooth, rounded hills on the landscape, called drumlins. Bunker Hill in Charlestown and some of the islands in Boston Harbor are drumlins.

Kettle ponds

As a glacier melts, big pieces of the ice may break off, and the meltwater flowing out from the glacier may deposit gravel, small rocks and other debris around the still unmelted chunk of ice, burying or surrounding it. When the chunk finally does melt, it can create a pond in the outwash plain called a kettle pond. Walden Pond in Concord and many of the ponds on Cape Cod are kettle ponds.

Ice age detectives

When a glacier melts, it leaves behind nothing of itself to tell geologists how it advanced. It does leave indirect clues, though. As a glacier advances over the land, it carries rocks in its bottom layers that scratch the exposed bedrock over which the ice passes. Atop Mount Washington in New Hampshire, the highest peak in New England at more than a mile above sea level, geologists have found scratch marks on exposed bedrock that they know to be evidence that a glacier passed over the mountain peak. That tells them the ice was at least that high in places.

As a glacier advances, it picks up rocks in one area and drops them in another. The rocks are erratics. Occasionally, the ice picks up bits of bedrock in an area with a kind of bedrock found almost nowhere else in that region. By mapping where these erratics are dropped, a scattering of rocks called a boulder train, geologists can tell the direction the glacier traveled. For instance, in Hatfield, Mass., there is an area of igneous bedrock, monzodiorite.

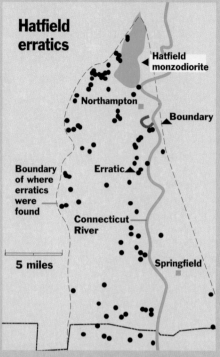

Hatfield erratics

Hatfield monzodiorite

Northampton

Boundary

Boundary of where erratics were found

Erratic

Connecticut River

5 miles

Springfield

Rocks of this type have been found in a fan-shaped area that extends nearly 20 miles to the south, marking the path of the glacier through that region.

New England's stone walls

If you've ever hiked in remote areas of New England, you know that miles of stone walls can run through the most isolated meadows and primitive forests in the region. It's an astonishing mystery if you don't know the explanation. Who could have sweated and toiled to construct lines of carefully stacked rocks running from nowhere to nowhere? The answer is: the region's earliest European farmers.

Much of New England was once covered with farm fields, but many of those farms were abandoned in the years after the American Civil War, and the fields have since grown back to forests. But when those early European farmers went to clear their land to plant crops, what they found were rocks and boulders, the debris dropped by New England's last glacier as it melted away.

So the region's stone walls were permanent fences around fields, but they were also trash piles for all those rocks and boulders. In 1871, the U.S. Department of Agriculture decided to count how many miles of stone fences there were in the nation. It turned out there were more miles of stone walls in the Northeast then than there are miles of railroad tracks in the entire country today.

Native Americans

The first Americans were probably a small band of big-game hunters, out in search of woolly mammoths, mastodons or caribou, who had no idea they were about to discover a vast new continent.

During the last ice age, so much of the earth's water was still ice that the oceans were more than a hundred feet lower than they are today. As a result, a temporary land bridge opened up connecting Siberia to Alaska. Human beings had already spread through much of Europe, Africa and Asia, but North America was still an uninhabited continent.

The earliest Americans entering Alaska, and those who followed them, continued to move down through Canada, finding an open passage between the great sheets of

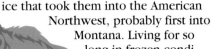

Hunting a woolly mammoth

ice that took them into the American Northwest, probably first into Montana. Living for so long in frozen conditions, they must have been startled as they continued to travel south and east and began to encounter warmer temperatures and the vast forests and fields of America's heartland.

Exactly when the first human beings arrived in North America is unclear. In the 1920s, stone arrowheads were found near Clovis, New Mexico, that date back to about 11,500 years ago. Sites in Alaska have been found that date back 12,000 years.

Far to the south, though, near Monte Verde, Chile, stone tools were found that date back to about 12,500 years ago. Some archaeologists believe that finding a human settlement in South America may mean human beings entered Alaska 20,000 or even 30,000 years ago. However, others say humans could have moved much faster down the North American coast.

Nevertheless, the glacial ice did not begin to melt away from the Northeast until 18,500 years ago, so hunters did not enter this region until after that.

The first arrivals in North America, whom we now call "Paleoindians," which means the oldest Indians, probably had lives many people today would envy. After all, many may have had a wealth of food, land to live on and leisure time.

Were they savages? Not at all, say anthropologists. They were just as intelligent and inventive as peo-

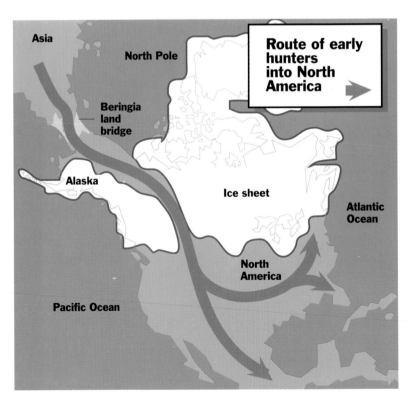

Asia

North Pole

Route of early hunters into North America

Beringia land bridge

Alaska

Ice sheet

Atlantic Ocean

North America

Pacific Ocean

ple today. Human beings have probably been thinking at our modern level of complexity for the past 50,000 years. That means there was just as much genius among these early people as there is among modern humans. There was also just as much greed, charity, cruelty and compassion then as now.

It's true that life for humans has changed dramatically over the centuries as their inventions and discoveries have accumulated. But their basic emotional and intellectual makeup has changed very little. If these early human cultures did not advance much beyond the use of simple tools, it's because there was little need for them to advance. By many standards, they were "rich" people. Their needs could be easily met. Indeed, they may have enjoyed life as much, if not more, than most people today.

Paleoindians were primarily nomads following the migration paths of the herd animals or the waterfowl, such as ducks and geese, that they hunted. They also fished and trapped small game animals such as beavers and rabbits.

They may have carried their limited belongings on sleds or toboggans drawn by domesticated dogs or pulled by members of the group. Their tools included hammers, chisels, axes and awls (hole makers) made from rock, as well as other implements, such as sewing needles, made from bones or the ivory of mammoth tusks.

The sewing needle dates back at least 40,000 years. So the first Americans probably wore tailored clothes of furs and skins. And they probably lived in tents made of skins that had been loosely sewn together.

They would camp, possibly for weeks or months at a time, near where animals were known to seek food or water, for instance in the flood plain of a river, near a forest opening or around ponds and other

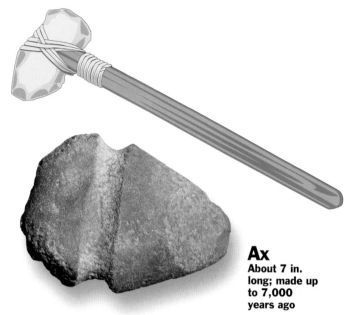

Ax
About 7 in. long; made up to 7,000 years ago

wetlands. They also gathered and ate fruits, berries, nuts and some plants. In fact, plant matter made up most of their diet. They would eventually move on, but if the hunting, fishing and berry picking were good enough, they might return to the same spot the next season.

The earliest residents of the Northeast probably had rich spiritual and social lives. Studies of modern-day hunting and gathering societies, such as those discovered in tropical rain forests, show they can be masters of conversation. Without television and books, they have talk as their main source of entertainment and information.

Paleoindians may have had larger vocabularies than many people today, especially for things in their natural surroundings, for types of plants, animals and weather conditions. They also relied on speech to pass along the knowledge accumulated over thousands of years – effective herbal cures, tips for hunting game, and designs of tents or layouts of camps.

It is likely they passed their abundant leisure time doing beadwork or other crafts, playing with wooden toys or games, singing and dancing, and just absorbing the beautiful unspoiled scenery.

As the population of

Fishing line

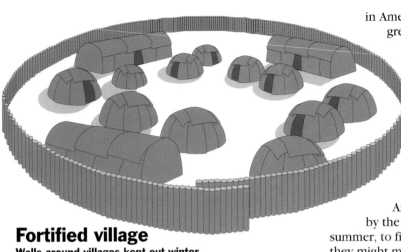

Fortified village

Walls around villages kept out winter winds as well as intruders.

Paleoindians grew in a region, it is also likely many families came together at certain times of the year for festivals where goods were traded, stories swapped and marriages arranged.

Certainly, medicine was not as advanced as it is today. But the simplicity of that era offered its own protection. The level of stress was probably very low. With so much food and land, war was probably not yet common, although personal arguments and hostilities have always existed.

And while more babies died in infancy than die today, those who survived childhood could often live into their forties or fifties. Native Americans did not suffer many of the diseases and medical problems that are now widespread, such as obesity, diabetes and high blood pressure, which often result from inactive lives and diets high in fat.

Indeed, when the first Europeans arrived in America, they were struck by the great health Native Americans seemed to enjoy.

What was life like for the Native Americans of the Northeast?

In many respects, it was simple. And it was cyclical. It had the seasons as its clock .

Five centuries ago, before Europeans settled in the region, many Native American families would live by the seashore or a riverbank in summer, to fish and to farm. In winter, they might move to protected inland areas to hunt squirrels, beavers, deer, moose or bears and to live off stored supplies of vegetables, nuts and berries.

Crops included maize (corn), beans, squash, pumpkins, cucumbers and tobacco. Villages sat beside the agricultural fields. Individual homes, called wigwams or wetus, were made of frameworks of branches that were covered with bark or with woven mats.

Usually, one family would live in each house. The sachem, or chief, often occupied a larger wigwam near the center of the village. A protected fence might be built around the edge of the village so that it could be a winter home or a fort.

To create open spaces for farming and for footpaths, Native Americans of New England would periodically burn over the land, destroying the underbrush and many of the trees. The practice would also create more open land for hunting, and it would kill off insect pests near villages.

Common foods included small cakes

World events

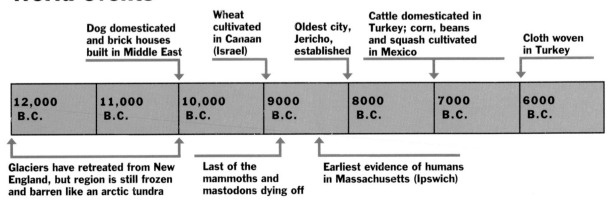

	Dog domesticated and brick houses built in Middle East	Wheat cultivated in Canaan (Israel)	Oldest city, Jericho, established	Cattle domesticated in Turkey; corn, beans and squash cultivated in Mexico		Cloth woven in Turkey
12,000 B.C.	11,000 B.C.	10,000 B.C.	9000 B.C.	8000 B.C.	7000 B.C.	6000 B.C.

Glaciers have retreated from New England, but region is still frozen and barren like an arctic tundra

Last of the mammoths and mastodons dying off

Earliest evidence of humans in Massachusetts (Ipswich)

New England events

made from ground corn as well as stews of meat, fish, nuts and vegetables. As treats, Native Americans ate popcorn and maple sugar. Tribes living along the coast also had clambakes, at which clams, fish and vegetables covered with seaweed would be baked atop fire-heated rocks.

Wigwams or wetus

Bark or woven mats were laid over frames made of branches. A hole in the roof allowed smoke from fires to escape.

Native American women were responsible for raising children, preparing meals and tending the crops and the home. Men were hunters, warriors and craftsmen, making the tools, utensils and weapons needed for survival. However, it is probable that these roles were often shared by men and women.

Native American children, especially boys, were encouraged at a young age to be bold and self-reliant. To prove he had reached manhood, a young male might be led blindfolded into the woods in winter, armed with a bow and arrow, a knife and a hatchet, and be expected to survive on his own until spring.

The most common clothing for both men and women in warm weather was the breech clout, a belt and cloth that performed the same function as a pair of shorts does today. In colder weather, sewn layers of animal skins were worn, often of raccoon or fox, with the fur side of the skin against the body.

Although most historians believe Native Americans were relatively peace-loving, as their population in New England grew and competition for land and resources increased, intertribal hostilities sometimes occurred.

Warfare had its own rituals and regulations, however. The night before an attack, a war dance might be held by the attacking tribe during which the enemy would be denounced for whatever had been done to deserve the hostility. There would also be tributes to the bravery of the tribe's own warriors, who would be covered in war paint. A warning would usually be given to the village about to be attacked.

Often launched at dawn, the attack might begin with a volley of arrows and then develop into hand-to-hand combat.

When the first Europeans arrived in the region in the early 1600s, there may have been an Native American population in New England of 150,000 to 200,000 people. However, diseases contracted from the earliest European trappers and traders – smallpox, measles, influenza, typhoid fever and tuberculosis – killed many

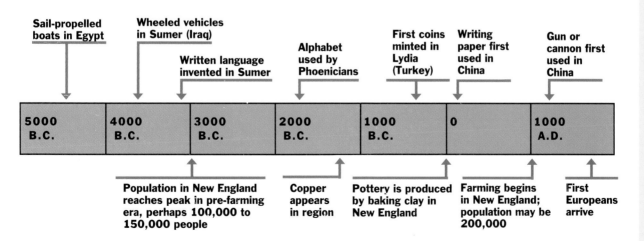

Sail-propelled boats in Egypt	Wheeled vehicles in Sumer (Iraq)	Written language invented in Sumer	Alphabet used by Phoenicians	First coins minted in Lydia (Turkey)	Writing paper first used in China	Gun or cannon first used in China
5000 B.C.	**4000 B.C.**	**3000 B.C.**	**2000 B.C.**	**1000 B.C.**	**0**	**1000 A.D.**
	Population in New England reaches peak in pre-farming era, perhaps 100,000 to 150,000 people		Copper appears in region	Pottery is produced by baking clay in New England	Farming begins in New England; population may be 200,000	First Europeans arrive

Native Americans. They had no history of these new illnesses and little or no immunity to them.

The first epidemic of the European diseases, believed to include smallpox, probably occurred in 1615, mainly affecting tribes along the New England coast. A second severe outbreak occurred in the early 1630s, reaching inland groups all the way to Canada.

Up to 95 percent of the Native Americans in some areas were killed during the epidemics. By the late 1630s, it is estimated that only 20,000 Native Americans remained alive in all of New England.

The French explorer Samuel de Champlain sailed down the New England coast in 1605, before the first epidemic, and described thriving farming villages filled with people all along the coast. Then, in 1620, when the Pilgrims land-

ed, they described in journals nearly abandoned villages with only a few people to be seen, untended fields, and skeletons left unburied on the ground.

At first, Native American populations and the colonists managed to live in relative peace. But as colonists increasingly bought up Native American lands, often by convincing tribes to sign contracts for sales they did not fully understand, tensions between the two groups increased.

Small skirmishes and other incidents occurred periodically. Then in 1675, King Philip's War broke out, and in the course of it the English permanently established their dominance in New England.

By the war's end in 1676, Native Americans had been driven out of much of New England, ending a way of life that had existed for them in the region for nearly a hundred centuries.

Crafting tools and weapons

Native Americans hunted game animals with spears and arrows and cleaned them with knives. The points on these tools and weapons were often made from chert, a type of rock that is also called flint. When chert was tapped with a sharp rock or other hard tool, flat flakes would come loose, allowing the rock to be chiseled into the desired shape. Once the point was finished, it might be inserted into a notch cut into a stick and then tied into place with animal tendons, leather strips or other strong, stringy material.

Spear point
Made 5,000 to 6,000 years ago

Arrowhead
Made 500 to 2,000 years ago

Knife point
Made 5,000 to 7,000 years ago

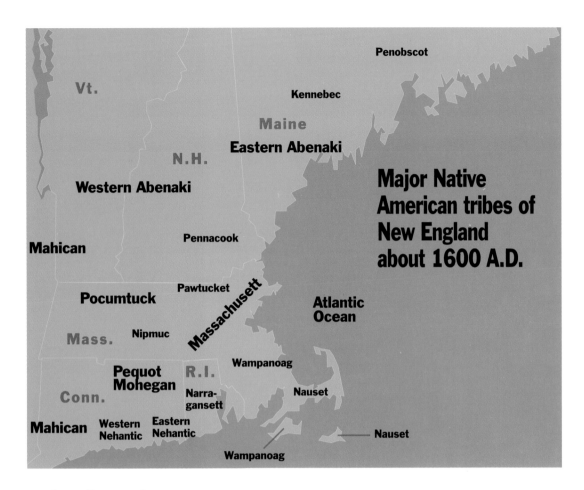

Penobscot

Vt.

Kennebec

Maine

N.H.

Eastern Abenaki

Western Abenaki

Major Native American tribes of New England about 1600 A.D.

Mahican

Pennacook

Pawtucket

Pocumtuck

Massachusett

Atlantic Ocean

Mass.

Nipmuc

Pequot
Mohegan

R.I.

Wampanoag

Conn.

Narra-
gansett

Nauset

Mahican

Western
Nehantic

Eastern
Nehantic

Nauset

Wampanoag

Archaeology in Eastern Massachusetts

Archaeologists are faced with a difficult task when they try to reconstruct the early history of humans in New England. Very little that is not rock has survived from ancient times because of New England's acidic ground water. In most cases, bones, fabrics, clay pottery and carved wood have long since disintegrated.

Despite all this, much about life for early human beings in the region is known. From the stone tools and the rock forma-tions of campsites, as well as the charcoal remains of campfires that are sometimes found, archaeologists are able to guess what animals those who lived in the camps were hunting, what their living quarters were like and whether they lived in large or small communities. They are able to estimate how old the campsite is within a few hundred years by using a technique called radiocarbon dating to

estimate the age of the charcoal.

The earliest evidence of human beings in Massachusetts comes from a site in Ipswich, called Bull Brook, that is at least 10,400 years old. Knives, scrapers, drills and other tools as well as projectile points, beaver and caribou bones, and charcoal fragments were found there. The site may have been an encampment for many families.

Along the Taunton River, archaeologists discovered a base camp for hunters dating back at least 8,000 years. A site more than 10,000 years old was found in Canton. And at sites from later eras, copper beads, soapstone bowls, smoking pipes, flutes, whistles, arrowheads, spear points, axes and pottery were unearthed.

The remains of houses and small villages were discovered around Assawompsett Pond in Lakeville and on Martha's Vineyard. In Boston, along the Charles River, archaeologists found the remains of a fishing weir – a fencelike trap built across the river into which fish would swim – that is more than 3,000 years old.

Mountains

Some of the world's most magnificent mountains were once found in New England. But that was hundreds of millions of years ago. All those years of rain and wind and the freeze and thaw of water in their crevices have steadily eroded these peaks. Today, New England's mountains are minor when compared with mountains in other parts of the world.

There are 30 states with mountains that rise higher above sea level than the tallest in Massachusetts, Mount Greylock in Adams. And Mount Greylock, at 3,491 feet above sea level, is less than an eighth the height of the world's tallest mountain, Mount Everest. The highest peak in New England, at 6,288 feet, is

Mount Washington in New Hampshire.

Eastern Massachusetts is primarily a coastal region, and so it has few high peaks. East of the Connecticut River, the highest peak is Wachusett Mountain in Princeton at 2,006 feet above sea level.

Just as the average daily temperature changes the farther north you travel in New England, it also changes the higher you go in elevation above sea level. In fact, the temperature falls by about 5°F every 1,000 feet you climb up a mountain. That means that the kinds of animals and plants, as well as the general weather conditions found near the peak of a tall mountain, are going to be different from those found at the base of the mountain.

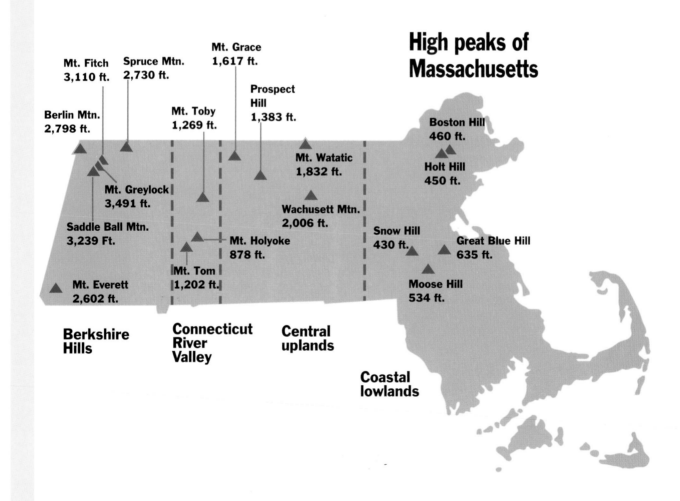

High peaks of Massachusetts

Mt. Fitch 3,110 ft.

Spruce Mtn. 2,730 ft.

Mt. Grace 1,617 ft.

Berlin Mtn. 2,798 ft.

Mt. Toby 1,269 ft.

Prospect Hill 1,383 ft.

Boston Hill 460 ft.

Mt. Greylock 3,491 ft.

Mt. Watatic 1,832 ft.

Holt Hill 450 ft.

Saddle Ball Mtn. 3,239 Ft.

Wachusett Mtn. 2,006 ft.

Snow Hill 430 ft.

Great Blue Hill 635 ft.

Mt. Holyoke 878 ft.

Mt. Everett 2,602 ft.

Mt. Tom 1,202 ft.

Moose Hill 534 ft.

Berkshire Hills

Connecticut River Valley

Central uplands

Coastal lowlands

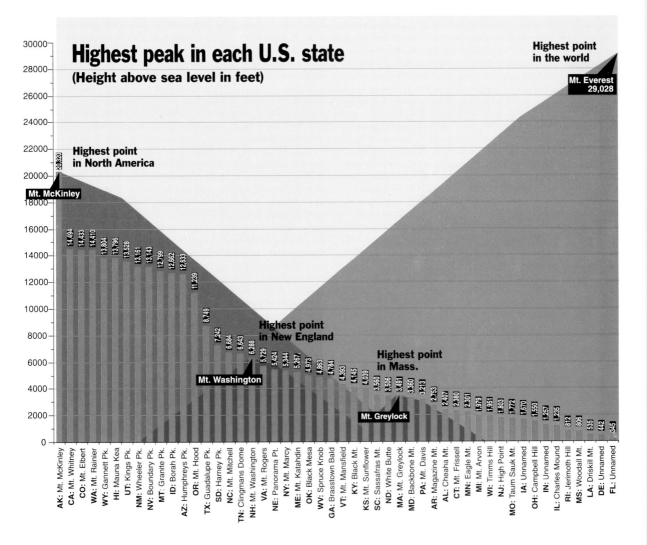

Highest peak in each U.S. state
(Height above sea level in feet)

Highest point in the world

Mt. Everest 29,028

Highest point in North America

20,320

Mt. McKinley

AK: Mt. McKinley	
CA: Mt. Whitney	14,494
CO: Mt. Elbert	14,433
WA: Mt. Rainier	14,410
WY: Gannett Pk.	13,804
HI: Mauna Kea	13,796
UT: Kings Pk.	13,528
NM: Wheeler Pk.	13,161
NV: Boundary Pk.	13,143
MT: Granite Pk.	12,799
ID: Borah Pk.	12,662
AZ: Humphreys Pk.	12,633
OR: Mt. Hood	11,239
TX: Guadalupe Pk.	8,749
SD: Harney Pk.	7,242
NC: Mt. Mitchell	6,684
TN: Clingmans Dome	6,643
NH: Mt. Washington	6,288
VA: Mt. Rogers	5,729
NE: Panorama Pt.	5,424
NY: Mt. Marcy	5,344
ME: Mt. Katahdin	5,267
OK: Black Mesa	4,973
WV: Spruce Knob	4,863
GA: Brasstown Bald	4,784
VT: Mt. Mansfield	4,393
KY: Black Mt.	4,145
KS: Mt. Sunflower	4,039
SC: Sassafras Mt.	3,560
ND: White Butte	3,506
MA: Mt. Greylock	3,491
MD: Backbone Mt.	3,360
PA: Mt. Davis	3,213
AR: Magazine Mt.	2,753
AL: Cheaha Mt.	2,407
CT: Mt. Frissell	2,380
MN: Eagle Mt.	2,301
MI: Mt. Arvon	1,979
WI: Timms Hill	1,951
NJ: High Point	1,803
MO: Taum Sauk Mt.	1,772
IA: Unnamed	1,670
OH: Campbell Hill	1,550
IN: Unnamed	1,257
IL: Charles Mound	1,235
RI: Jerimoth Hill	812
MS: Woodall Mt.	806
LA: Driskill Mt.	535
DE: Unnamed	442
FL: Unnamed	345

Highest point in New England

Mt. Washington

Highest point in Mass.

Mt. Greylock

Atop Mount Washington, where on a clear day you can see five states and Canada, there are no birds during winter, except for the occasional visit of a scavenger raven. At about 4,000 feet above sea level on the mountain's slopes – the elevation called the timberline – trees can no longer grow. Above that level, the only plants are species usually found much farther north in the colder regions of Canada. The only animals above Mount Washington's timberline may be shrews, voles and an occasional weasel.

At the top of Mount Washington, the average daily temperature in July is about 48°F. In Boston, which is near sea level, the average daily temperature that time of year is about 74°F.

In January, you can expect an average temperature on Mount Washington of about 4°F, while in Boston the average temperature is about 30°F.

Boston gets an average of about 41 inches of snow a year. The peak of Mount Washington gets some 255 inches of snow annually.

The strongest winds you might experience in Boston in any year might be about 60 miles per hour. But atop Mount Washington in winter, on most days the winds reach hurricane force, 74 miles per hour. In fact, in April, 1934, winds at the summit reached 231 miles per hour, the fastest winds that had ever been recorded on earth.

Water

You never have to travel far in Massachusetts to find water. With more than 2,000 rivers and streams as well as nearly 900 lakes and ponds, not to mention the Atlantic Ocean on its coast, Massachusetts has water, water everywhere – and quite a lot to drink.

Most people think of the Pacific Northwest as America's rain capital. In fact, Seattle gets less rainfall each year (an average of 38.8 inches) than Boston (43.8 inches).

The presence of so much water gives the state a great diversity of wildlife. There is a long list of plants and animals that live only in water, and another long list of wildlife that live alongside water.

The land surface of Massachusetts slopes from the Berkshire Hills on the west to the Atlantic Coast on the east. It also slopes toward Long Island Sound on the south. These gradual slopes have produced one group of rivers that flow generally east, such as the Merrimack River, and another set that flow generally south, such as the Taunton River.

A half century ago, many of the state's major rivers were polluted eyesores because of the sewage, chemicals and trash that were being dumped into them. But citizen and government action to clean up these waterways, including the construction of sewage treatment plants, has turned many of them into clean rivers.

In 1970, the Nashua River was one of the nation's 10 most polluted rivers, and only 5 percent of the land forming its banks was protected. Today, you can safely swim and fish in the Nashua, and

Dreamed Brook, Littleton

more than 65 percent of its banks are protected.

The drinking water of Eastern Massachusetts comes primarily from two manmade lakes – the Quabbin Reservoir in Belchertown and the Wachusett Reservoir in Boylston. They are connected to Boston and other eastern communities by massive underground pipes, or aqueducts. Quabbin Reservoir alone can hold 412 billion gallons of water when full.

Massachusetts has long valued its large lakes and ponds. In colonial times, those

Lake or pond?

● The usual definition of a pond is that it is shallow enough for aquatic plants to grow anywhere in it. But a lake can be so deep and dark in places that plants only grow in the shallow areas.

over 10 acres in surface area, called great ponds, were made community property by law, which meant that the state actually owned the land beneath them.

Many of the state's rivers and lakes have kept the names Native Americans gave them. One is Lake Chargoggagoggmanchaugagoggchaubunagungamuagg in Webster. To Native Americans, that meant "You fish on your side, we fish on our side, and nobody fishes in the middle." Many people today also call it Webster Lake.

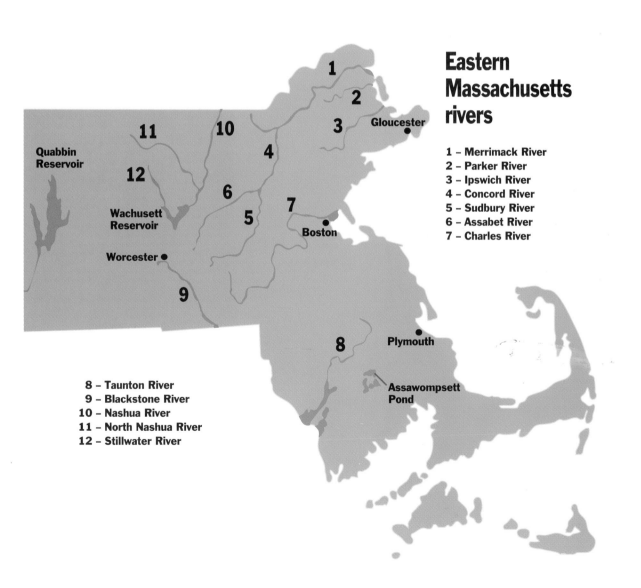

Eastern Massachusetts rivers

1 – Merrimack River
2 – Parker River
3 – Ipswich River
4 – Concord River
5 – Sudbury River
6 – Assabet River
7 – Charles River

8 – Taunton River
9 – Blackstone River
10 – Nashua River
11 – North Nashua River
12 – Stillwater River

Merrimack River

Source – Near Franklin, N.H.
Mouth – Atlantic Ocean
River length – 134 miles through N.H. and Mass.
River length in Mass. – 45.2 miles
Total area drained in Mass. – 1,210 square miles

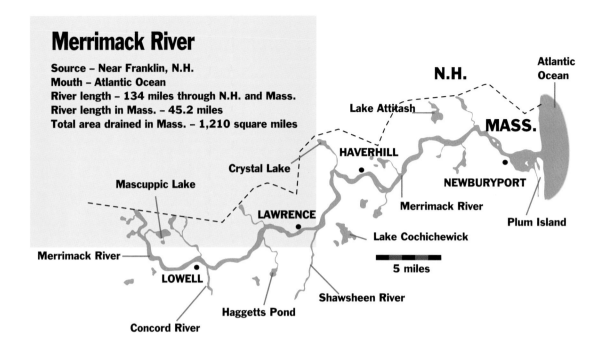

N.H.

Atlantic Ocean

Lake Attitash

MASS.

Crystal Lake

HAVERHILL

NEWBURYPORT

Mascuppic Lake

Merrimack River

Plum Island

Merrimack River

LAWRENCE

Lake Cochichewick

5 miles

LOWELL

Shawsheen River

Concord River

Haggetts Pond

Concord, Assabet and Sudbury river system

Sources
  Concord – Assabet and Sudbury rivers
  Assabet – Mill Pond in Westborough
  Sudbury – Cedar Swamp in Westborough
Mouths
  Concord – Merrimack River
  Assabet – Concord River
  Sudbury – Concord River
River lengths in Mass.
  Concord – 15.5 miles
  Assabet – 29.8 miles
  Sudbury – 28.8 miles
Total area drained by the three rivers –
  377 square miles

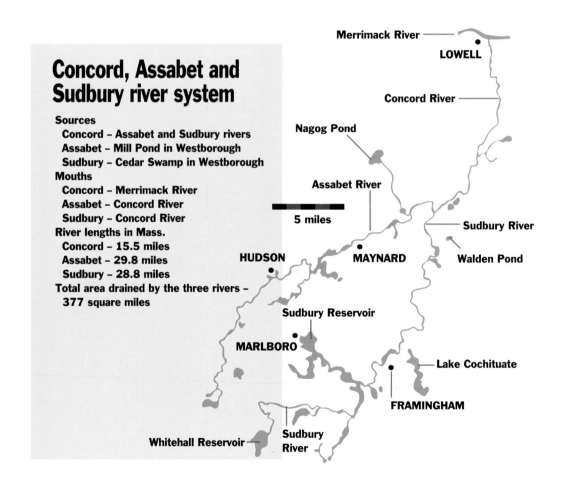

Merrimack River

LOWELL

Concord River

Nagog Pond

Assabet River

Sudbury River

Walden Pond

5 miles

HUDSON

MAYNARD

Sudbury Reservoir

MARLBORO

Lake Cochituate

FRAMINGHAM

Whitehall Reservoir

Sudbury River

Charles River

Source – A spring in Hopkinton
Mouth – Boston Harbor
River length in Mass. – 80 miles
Total area drained in Mass. –
307 square miles

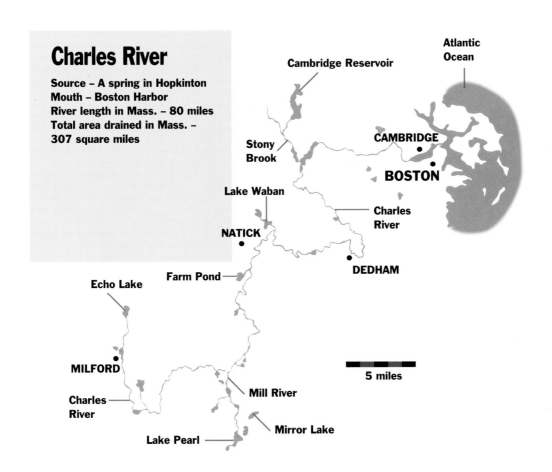

Cambridge Reservoir

Atlantic Ocean

Stony Brook

CAMBRIDGE

BOSTON

Lake Waban

Charles River

NATICK

DEDHAM

Echo Lake

Farm Pond

MILFORD

Charles River

Mill River

Mirror Lake

Lake Pearl

5 miles

Nashua River

Source – Wachusett Reservoir
Mouth – Merrimack River
River length – 56 miles
River length in Mass. – 46 miles
Total area drained in Mass. –
454 square miles

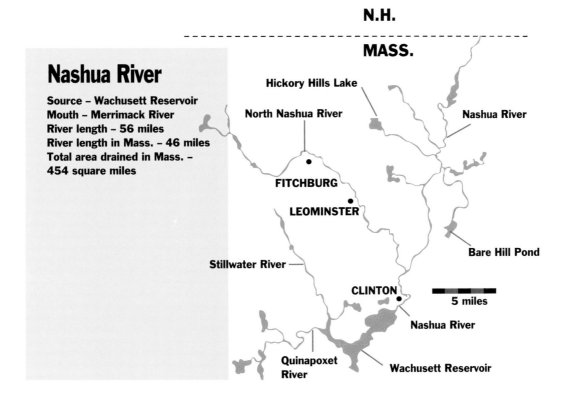

N.H.

- -

MASS.

Hickory Hills Lake

North Nashua River

Nashua River

FITCHBURG

LEOMINSTER

Bare Hill Pond

Stillwater River

CLINTON

5 miles

Nashua River

Quinapoxet River

Wachusett Reservoir

Aquifers

If it's true, as Ben Franklin said, that people don't know the value of water until the well runs dry, then most New Englanders will never know what a sparkling glass of water is actually worth.

Water, in the form of rain or snow, falls in abundance in this region. Much of it is stored below ground in aquifers, a gift of the last ice age.

Aquifers are areas where water collects and does not drain away. An aquifer might be an area of loose stone or sand that sits atop a depressed area of solid rock through which water can't pass. When water seeps into such an area, the solid rock acts like the sides and bottom of a swimming pool, trapping the water.

Aquifers might also be areas of porous rock – rock with holes and hollow places in it – that trap water. Or they can be faults or breaks between solid areas of bedrock, underground crevices that store water. The water that aquifers hold is pumped to the surface through wells.

In Massachusetts, aquifers are often buried valleys dug out by glaciers that came through New England. When water turns to ice, its volume expands. And on the edge of a glacier, water will seep into bedrock crevices, expand when it freezes, and then crack apart the rock the way that ice in the winter cracks apart cement sidewalks and asphalt roads. Eventually, this process will dig valleys or crevices in bedrock.

When glaciers melt, all the loose sand, gravel and bits of rock that had been frozen into the ice get dropped to the ground. This material can fill up the valleys the glacier formed in the bedrock, creating ideal future aquifers.

Aquifers exist in all parts of the country, but in areas with low rainfall, such as in the U.S. Southwest, some aquifers can run dry if too much water is drawn out of them.

In New England, the main threat to the ground water is pollution. Just a gallon of gasoline seeping into an aquifer can pollute a million gallons of water.

Massachusetts has some of the strongest laws in the nation to protect its drinking water supplies from pollution.

Wetlands

Between dry land and the deep water of lakes, rivers or the ocean you will often see wetlands, areas where land and water mix. Swamps, marshes and bogs are wetlands, as are wet meadows and riverbank forests that may flood after heavy rains.

Wetlands were once considered places of no value in much of America. In fact, in the last two centuries more than half the acreage of wetlands in the lower 48 states has been filled, dredged, drained or otherwise lost so that the land could be used for other purposes.

But wetlands do have great value, people have learned. They filter out pollution before it reaches larger bodies of water, they hold excess water in times of flood, and they are home to many kinds of plants and animals, from cattails to muskrats, that are seen almost nowhere else. That's why wetlands are now protected by law.

Since 1780 in Massachusetts, nearly 28 percent of the state's wetlands have disappeared, most of them inland freshwater wetlands. The state now has about half a million acres of freshwater and saltwater wetlands.

Muskrat

Quinapoxet River, Holden

Endangered wildlife

A little more than a century ago, America was not a land where the deer and the antelope played or the buffalo roamed. Populations of these animals and many others had been reduced in places to the point that the survival of many species was very much in doubt.

Similarly, parts of the Northeast were nearly barren of wildlife that had lived there for thousands of years – black bears, moose, beavers and bald eagles.

The cutting of forests, plowing of meadows, damming of rivers and unrestricted commercial hunting had taken their toll on wildlife.

To halt the decline in animal populations, laws that regulated hunting were established in many states in the early 1900s. This worked well for some animals, such as black bears and white-tailed deer, which gradually returned on their own to forested areas they had once inhabited.

In the case of animals that did not return on their own, wildlife biologists tried to raise them on game farms for release into the wild, or they captured wild animals in other states or even other countries for release locally.

However, it was not enough to return these once-native animals to their historic territories. Their habitats – the land and water – also had to be restored. Loss of habitat is the reason most species of plants and animals become rare or endangered. So thousands of acres of forests were bought to establish state and federal forests, parks and wildlife refuges. And rivers that had been fouled with sewage and trash were gradually cleaned up.

If animals were to be restored in Massachusetts, they also had to be protected. In 1973, the federal Endangered Species Act was passed, making it a crime to hunt or otherwise harm many species of rare animals and plants. In addition, in most states, including Massachusetts, laws were passed to protect animals or plants that were rare or endangered in that state.

State laws were also passed to protect wetland areas, such as ponds, lakes, marshes and rivers. Animals depend on water for survival, and areas where land and water come together, such as the land surrounding a stream or river, are among the most productive habitats for plants and animals. Red-winged blackbirds and marsh wrens nest in the cattails of pond edges. Moose and black bears feed on vegetation found in swamps and marshes. And muskrats and river otters live in water, making their dens along the banks of streams and rivers.

Bald eagle, endangered in Massachusetts

Massachusetts' endangered species

Massachusetts has more than 400 species of native plants and animals that are endangered, threatened or of special concern in the state. A species is endangered if it is on the verge of extinction in its natural range. It is threatened if it is on the verge of being endangered. It is of special concern if it is becoming rare in its range. It is on the federal endangered species list if it is endangered or threatened nationwide. It is on the state list if it is endangered, threatened or of special concern in Massachusetts even though it may be more common in other states.

	Native species	Endangered state list / federal list	Threatened state list / federal list	Special concern state list	Total state list / federal list
Mammals	91	7/7	0/0	5	12/7
Birds [1]	209	12/3	6/2	11	29/5
Reptiles	30	8/4	5/3	3	16/7
Amphibians	21	0/0	2/0	4	6/0
Fish (inland only)	39	4/1	2/0	4	10/1
Invertebrates [2]	Not Known	26/2	18/2	61	105/4
Plants	1,650	119/2	79/1	53	251/3
Total [3]	2,040	176/19	112/8	141	429/27

[1] Includes only native bird species known to nest in Massachusetts and not the 90 or so species that pass through the state while migrating
[2] Includes butterflies, moths, beetles, dragonflies, crustaceans, mussels, snails, worms and sponges
[3] Excludes invertebrates

Federal endangered species list includes these Mass. natives:

Shortnose sturgeon
Plymouth redbelly turtle
Roseate tern
Humpback whale
American burying beetle
Northeastern bulrush

State endangered species list includes:

All Mass. species on the federal list
Atlantic sturgeon
Upland sandpiper
Northern copperhead
Short-eared owl
Puritan tiger beetle
Eastern silvery aster

Showy lady's slipper, endangered in Massachusetts.

Birds

From northern cardinals and black-capped chickadees to great horned owls and bald eagles, there thrives in the sky as large a population as on land.

In fact, a larger population. It's estimated there may be 20 times as many birds on earth as people. Walk through any field or forest in summer and you can easily believe it.

Nearly 300 species of birds can regularly be seen in the state, including more than 200 that have nested in Massachusetts. About 130 other species are seen occasionally in the state. In all of North America, more than 800 species of birds have been reported. And worldwide, there may be more than 9,000 different species of birds.

While large forests in the region attract their share of birds that seek isolation, such as scarlet tanagers and hermit thrushes, populated cities and suburbs are home to birds that can easily live around people, such as American goldfinches and mourning doves.

Nearly 140 million years ago, the first birds were appearing on earth. But they may have looked more like winged lizards than modern birds. Birds, like most creatures, have changed, or evolved, over millions of years to have specialized features that give them an advantage over other living things, the most important of which is the ability to fly and to live much of their lives above the ground and in the air.

Even among birds, though, different

Catbirds

species have evolved to have different features – variations in size, coloring, wing shape or body shape. Because of these physical differences, some birds can find food in ways that others can't, or they can live and nest in places where others can't. As a result, more kinds of birds can survive than would be possible if all birds ate the same foods and lived and nested in the same places.

Birds that are born with a slight difference that gives them an advantage in finding food, such as a slightly longer beak, or an

Canada goose chick

advantage in escaping predators, such as greater flying speed, are more likely to survive and have young. Therefore, their special features are more likely to be passed along to future generations.

Over millions of years, woodpeckers developed to have strong, sharp beaks, long tongues and sharp claws. They use their claws to grab onto the sides of trees, and they use their beaks to peck nest holes in trees and to dig beneath bark to find insects. They use their long tongues to grab the insects they find.

Hummingbirds developed to be very small (they are the smallest of all birds, sometimes weighing less than a penny)

and to have very strong wing muscles and long, thin beaks. They can beat their wings very rapidly, even as fast as 75 times each second, to hover at flowers like bumble bees, and they use their long beaks like drinking straws to sip the nectar inside flowers.

Herons and egrets developed to have long, thin legs and long, sharp beaks. They use their legs to wade in the shallow water of lakes, streams and ponds. They can stand very still and wait for a fish or tadpole to pass by so that they can spear it with their beaks. To a fish, their thin legs may look like reeds.

Because northern winters can be harsh and food can be scarce, most birds migrate in the fall to warmer regions in the southern United States and to Central and South America, and then they return in the spring.

One of the main migration routes for birds moving between their breeding grounds in Canada and northern New England and their wintering homes farther south follows the Massachusetts coast. On Plum Island in Newburyport, for instance, many non-native species of birds can be spotted each spring and fall as they pass

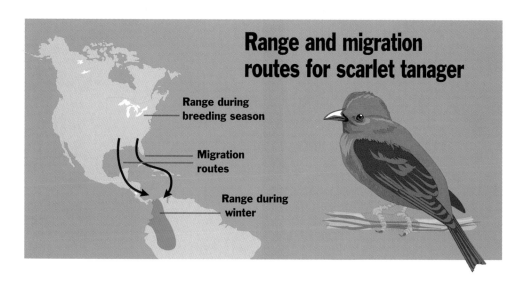

Range and migration routes for scarlet tanager

Range during breeding season

Migration routes

Range during winter

Northern cardinal

overhead or when they stop for a rest during their migration.

In Massachusetts, songbirds usually nest and lay their eggs in April, May and June. For smaller birds, like the tufted titmouse, white-breasted nuthatch and tree swallow, the eggs take about two weeks to hatch, and the young stay in the nest two to three weeks before they take

Is it a songbird?

● A songbird is the general name given to birds that perch on branches, such as sparrows, finches, cardinals and jays. However, some are not particularly good singers.

their first flights. For larger birds, such as great horned owls and red-tailed hawks, the eggs may take nearly four weeks to hatch, and the young may remain in the nest four to six weeks.

Birds in the wild have varying life spans. Harsh weather, accidents, disease and lack of food can take their toll. Most songbirds live only two to five years. However, some larger birds, such as mallards and great blue herons, may live 20 years or more.

Songs and calls

The songs and calls of birds are their language. They use these sounds to tell other birds a territory is theirs, to attract a mate and to warn of danger.

Their songs and calls may sound like this:

Tufted titmouse – "Peter! Peter! Peter!"

Great horned owl – "Who, who-who-who, who, who!"

Mourning dove – "Coo-ah, coo, coo, coo!"

Gray catbird – "Meow!"

Ovenbird – "Teacher, teacher, teacher!"

Rufous-sided towhee – "Drink your tea!"

Baltimore oriole – "Tea too!"

White-throated sparrow – "Poor Sam Peabody, Peabody, Peabody!"

American goldfinch – "Potato chip!"

Red-winged blackbird – "Ok-a-lee!"

Nesting birds of Massachusetts

Some birds will nest in residential areas. Shown for the birds below is: Nest construction – Average number of eggs per brood – Broods per season – Period during which eggs are laid – Time to hatching – Time to nestlings' first flights

Blue jay

A cup of rootlets, twigs, bark strips and leaves, usually in an evergreen tree 10 to 25 feet off the ground – Four or five eggs – One brood – April 28 to June 18 – About 17 days – 17 to 21 days

Black-capped chickadee

A cavity in a standing dead tree lined with cottony fibers, fur, moss, hair, wool and feathers, usually 4 to 10 feet off the ground – Six to eight eggs – One or two broods – May 4 to July 12 – About 12 days – About 16 days

Ruby-throated hummingbird

A small cup of plant down, fibers and spider silk built in the fork of a drooping limb, usually 10 to 20 feet off the ground – Two eggs – One brood – May 24 to July 22 – 11 to 16 days – 14 to 28 days

American robin

A deep cup made of grasses and weed stalks and shaped with mud in the fork of a tree branch, in shrubs or on a window ledge usually 5 to 15 feet off the ground – Three or four eggs – Two or three broods – April 12 to July 25 – About 12 days – About 15 days

Downy woodpecker

A cavity in a living or dead tree, usually 20 to 30 feet off the ground – Four or five eggs – One brood – May 20 to June 21 – About 12 days – About 21 days

Northern cardinal

A shallow cup of twigs, grasses, rootlets and vines in dense shrubs or thickets or in an evergreen tree, usually less than 10 feet off the ground – Three or four eggs – Two or three broods – Late April to late June – About 12 days – About 14 days

House sparrow

A cavity lined with grasses, weeds and feathers in a tree, on a building, on a billboard or in a birdhouse, usually 10 to 50 feet off the ground – Five eggs – Two or three broods – Feb. to Sept. – About 12 days – 13 to 18 days

American robin – 10 in. – Y* – Robins can often be seen standing on lawns, their heads cocked to one side, looking for their favorite food, earthworms.

Red-winged blackbird – 8.5 in. – B – "Redwings" nest in wetlands. The males often perch atop cat-tails, calling, ready to defend their territories.

Northern cardinal – 8.5 in. – Y – The red-colored male and the buff-colored female, shown here, can be frequent visitors to backyard feeders.

American goldfinch – 5 in. – Y – In summer, the male has a rich yellow color, which turns greenish yellow in winter, a color closer to that of the female.

Black-capped chickadee – 5 in. – Y – Chickadees are bold and curious birds. They will venture close to people, and they frequently visit feeders.

Tufted titmouse – 6 in. – Y – An acrobat, the tit-mouse will hang upside down on a branch, searching for insects in the bark and on the leaves.

* "Y" refers to a year-round resident of Massachusetts, "B" refers to a resident during the breeding season, and "W" refers to a resident during winter.

White-breasted nuthatch – 6 in. – Y – Nuthatches will travel headfirst down a tree, searching for insects in the bark. They nest in tree cavities.

Blue jay – 12 in. – Y – Jays have a noisy call, "Jay! Jay!" that gives them their names. Aggressive birds, they may push other birds aside at feeders.

European starling – 8 in. – Y – A flock of these European natives was released near New York City in 1890. They are now found across North America.

House sparrow – 6 in. – Y – Natives of Europe, a few house sparrows were released in New York in 1850. These sparrows are now found coast to coast.

Song sparrow – 6 in. – Y – Song sparrows have a song that may sound like "Madge, Madge, Madge, put on your tea kettle-ettle-ettle!"

White-throated sparrow – 7 in. – Y – This sparrow is often seen in winter, scratching the ground beneath bird feeders, searching for fallen seeds.

Baltimore oriole - 8 in.- B - Orioles build nests out of plant fibers and pieces of bark. The nests may look like deep baskets hanging high in trees.

House finch - 5.5 in. - Y - House finches, originally western U.S. birds, were introduced near New York City in the 1940s and have thrived in the East.

American crow - 19 in. - Y - Scavengers, crows will eat almost anything edible, from crops in fields to animals killed along the highway.

Common grackle - 12 in. - B - Grackles often travel in noisy flocks. Their eyes are yellow, and in sunlight their feathers are iridescent blue or purple.

Rock dove - 13 in. - Y - Commonly called pigeons, these doves are European natives that were brought to North America in the 1600s.

Dark-eyed junco - 6 in. - Y - Juncos are most often seen in winter, searching for seeds beneath feeders. They may spend the rest of the year in forests.

Mourning dove – 12 in. – Y – These doves get their name from their slow, mournful call, "Oo-who, who, who, who." They have up to five broods a year.

Evening grosbeak – 8 in.– W – Their strong beaks give grosbeaks their name. They may visit feeders in flocks in winter. The male is shown here on the left.

Tree swallow – 6 in. – B – These swallows are often seen sweeping back and forth through the air as they snare flying insects, their favorite food.

Northern mockingbird – 11 in. – Y – Mockingbirds are mimics, able to imitate the sounds of other birds, barking dogs, sirens and musical instruments.

Yellow warbler – 5 in. – B – These warblers, which nest close to swamps and marshes, arrive in breeding areas in late April and are gone by late July.

Canada goose – 38 in. – Y – While some migrate, many Canada geese stay in the region through the winter. They often feed on grass.

Cedar waxwing – 7 in. – Y – Elegantly colored, cedar waxwings like fruits and berries and are usually seen in orchards and gardens. They often travel in large flocks.

Hairy woodpecker – 9 in. – Y – This woodpecker is very similar in appearance to the downy woodpecker except that the downy is smaller – about 6 inches in length. The downy also has a smaller bill.

Eastern bluebird – 6.5 in. – B – Bluebirds are not as plentiful as they once were. They nest in tree cavities, which are used for nesting by an increasing number of other birds, including starlings.

House wren – 5 in.– B – Insect eaters, house wrens nest in small, protected openings, including birdhouses, mailboxes, and even shoes left outdoors.

Northern flicker – 13 in. – Y – Flickers are often seen on the ground in pastures, on lawns or in forest clearings searching for their favorite food, ants.

Ruby-throated hummingbird – 3.5 in. – B – The only hummingbird native to the eastern United States, the "rubythroat" will hover at flowers, sipping the sweet nectar inside with its long bill. The female is shown here.

Green heron - 20 in. - B - These small herons feed on a variety of insects, frogs, tadpoles and fish. They will sit in tree branches just over water or crouch on shore, waiting for prey to come within striking distance.

Great blue heron - 48 in. - Y - Great blue herons are wading birds that you might see standing motionless in ponds, ready to spear small fish or tadpoles with their long, sharp beaks.

Mallard - 23 in. - Y - Mallards are the most common ducks in North America. They nest in the tall grasses or reeds near water. "Quack! Quack!" is the call of the female, which is shown above.

Ring-billed gull - 19 in. - Y - These gulls are often seen around shopping centers, fastfood restaurants and landfills scavenging for food. They may gather in flocks in parking lots.

Great black-backed gull - 30 in. - Y - The largest gull in the world, the great black-backed gull is most often seen in coastal areas. It eats fish but also feeds on other birds, such as terns, and their eggs.

Snowy egret - 24 in. - B - Facing extinction a century ago because of demand for their beautiful feathers, snowy egrets are now protected and are once again common in coastal wetlands.

Raptors

Raptors are the royalty of the skies. Eagles, hawks, falcons, owls and other raptors have features that are standards of excellence in the animal world. Consider the sharp eyes of an eagle, the keen hearing of an owl or the breathtaking speed of a diving falcon. Throughout the Northeast, the populations of many species of these birds of prey are soaring.

It has become common now to see a red-tailed hawk sitting high in a roadside tree or an American kestrel perched on a telephone wire.

In the 1960s, though, some species of raptors were headed for extinction. A widely used chemical pesticide, DDT, caused them to lay eggs with no shells or shells so thin that they broke. DDT was banned in 1972, and almost immediately, populations of birds of prey began to recover.

In 1963, there were only 420 known pairs of nesting eagles in the lower 48

Great horned owl

states. Today, there are more than 5,000 pairs, including a pair nesting near Assawompsett Pond in Lakeville.

Many raptors have also been helped by changes in how land is used. A little more than a century ago, farm fields covered much of the Northeast, but many of those farms have been abandoned, and the fields have grown back to forests.

Today, the region has a rich mixture of landscapes – patches of forests that are alongside patches of meadows, farm fields or residential neighborhoods. And this change has helped many species, especially those that like to perch in trees on the edges of forests and hunt small animals in open areas, such as Cooper's hawks and red-tailed hawks.

However, a few species have been hurt by the changes, especially barn owls and northern harriers, which prefer farms and fields.

Red-tailed hawks at their nest

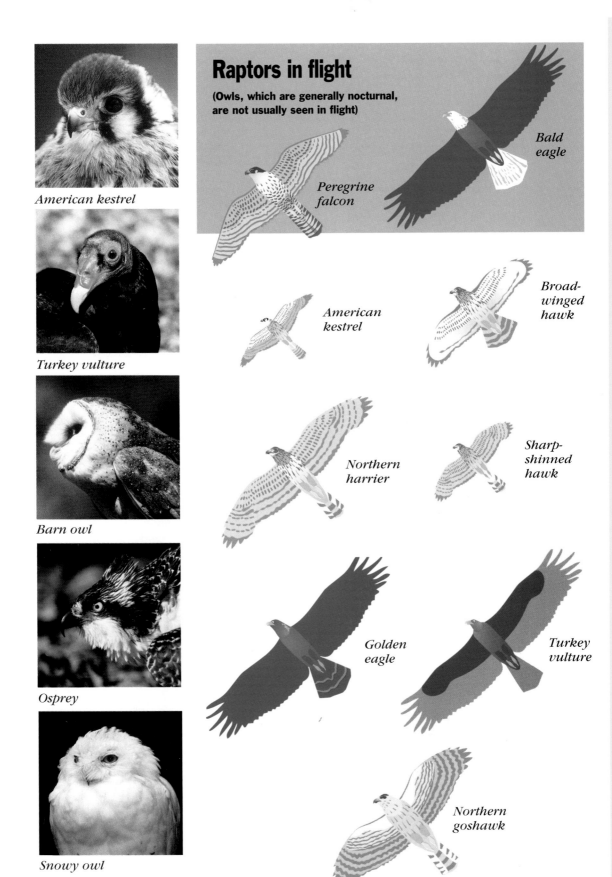

American kestrel

Turkey vulture

Barn owl

Osprey

Snowy owl

Raptors in flight

(Owls, which are generally nocturnal, are not usually seen in flight)

Peregrine falcon

Bald eagle

American kestrel

Broad-winged hawk

Northern harrier

Sharp-shinned hawk

Golden eagle

Turkey vulture

Northern goshawk

Deer

When a leaf falls in the forest, so the saying goes, an eagle will see it, a bear will smell it, and a deer will hear it.

Gifted with extremely sharp hearing, white-tailed deer are perhaps the ultimate forest animals. Far from the delicate creatures many people think them, deer are tough and hardy survivors. They use their hearing to avoid the few predators they have, and they can live close to residential neighborhoods while rarely being seen.

White-tailed deer, with their large brown eyes, white tails and sleek, athletic forms, can be a striking sight. In the wild, they may live seven years or more. The males (bucks) can reach 200 to 250 pounds in weight, and does may reach 150 to 175 pounds.

Bucks grow antlers each year and shed them in late winter. If food is plentiful, a doe may breed when she is six months old and have a fawn around her first birthday in the spring. In later years, she may have one to three fawns each spring, which means deer populations can grow rapidly.

Deer prefer areas where there are forests mixed with clearings, wetlands or abandoned pastures.

White-tailed deer

They are vegetarians, favoring the buds and twigs of young trees, but they will also eat nuts such as acorns. In residential areas, they like to nibble on shrubs and garden flowers.

Deer are swift runners, reaching speeds of 35 miles per hour. They are also able swimmers. In summer, bucks and does tend to live separately, but in winter, they may gather together.

In Massachusetts, there may be 80,000 to 90,000 white-tailed deer spread across the state, more than at any time in the last 150 years.

4–5 in. long

White-tailed deer

may gather in dense stands of evergreens, called "deer yards," in severe winters with deep snow. Snow depths are usually less there, and they can browse on the branches. The trees also give them protection from the wind, cold temperatures and blowing snow.

Moose

Moose disappeared from Massachusetts nearly two centuries ago, eliminated by hunting, the clearing of forests for farming, and the loss of beaver ponds. But these lumbering giants are gradually returning from northern New England, where they are still common, to take up residence in the state. There may now be several hundred moose in Massachusetts, many of them residents of northern Worcester County.

Moose

As slow-moving and harmless as moose can seem, though, they can pose a serious problem for people driving on highways. Moose are so large (they can grow to weigh a half ton or more) that they do not usually flee from danger, whether it's an approaching animal or an oncoming car. Moose will often hold their ground, and that can result in serious accidents when a car and a moose collide.

Moose can stand seven feet at the shoulder, and their impressive weight sits atop long, spindly legs. Moose are most likely to be seen near dawn and dusk when they are out foraging for food. They are most frequently seen between late August and November, when bulls are wandering farther than normally in search of mates. At that time of year, in areas where moose are found, you might hear the resounding bellows of bulls as they call to females.

A bull's massive rack of antlers, which can be five feet across, is shed each year in winter. As with all deer, the female does not grow antlers. On a moose, the antlers begin to grow in April and reach their full size by August.

Moose keep to themselves much of the time, feeding alone in forest clearings on the leaves, twigs and bark of trees. During summer, several may gather near ponds, bogs and lakes to feed on aquatic plants. During winter, groups of moose may gather in forest openings created by logging or in open areas beneath power lines to feed on the twigs of young trees. In the wild, moose can live up to 20 years.

8–9 in. long

Moose are often found around swamps and lakes, eating vegetation and submerging in the water to escape insects.

Bears

Yes, you can find lots of bears in the woods of Massachusetts – but not in the woods of Eastern Massachusetts, at least not yet.

During colonial times, black bears may have been as common as people, but by 1900 they were just about gone from the state, their numbers reduced primarily by year-round hunting and the clearing of forest lands for farming. With restrictions on bear hunting and the regrowth of many forests, black bears gradually moved back into most of Western Massachusetts.

However, now they have filled nearly all the territory that is suitable for them west of the Connecticut River, so young bears have started moving east, into Worcester County and beyond, to establish their own territories.

Black bears have long suffered from a public relations problem created by the larger, more aggressive grizzly and brown bears – neither of which is found anywhere near New England. The basic difference is that eastern black bears rarely attack human beings. And they generally won't attack unless they are defending a cub or have been surprised.

Black bears, which can live 25 years or more, are likely to weigh 150 to 250 pounds (although a few have reached more than 500 pounds). They eat what's available through the seasons but have a special taste for fruits, berries, acorns, beechnuts, apples, field corn, honey and

Black bear

even honey bee larvae. They will also come right into back yards to grab seeds out of bird feeders or to go through garbage cans for a meal.

Females give birth during hibernation every other year. They usually have two to four cubs at a time. The cubs will stay with the mother for more than a year, denning with her the following winter before going out on their own during their second year.

The hibernation itself is not the deep sleep most people imagine. In fact, cross-country skiers and winter hikers are occasionally startled by a bear they accidentally wake from sleep beside a trail when it suddenly rises from beneath a snow-covered tree and flees into the woods.

8 in. long

Black bears

will go into semi-hibernation from December to March or April of each year, living off their stored body fat. Their winter dens are built beneath fallen trees, in brush piles, in caves, and often in less hidden places, such as in the middle of a mountain laurel patch.

Coyotes

Brush wolves. Sagebrush scavengers. Coyotes might make you think of western prairies and haunting howls on moonlit nights.

But coyotes now reside near the hearts of many eastern cities, including Boston, prowling urban parks, passing themselves off to the casual observer as German shepherds or other large, bushy-tailed dogs.

Coyotes are recent arrivals in the Northeast, but they have already become common in the region. One theory is that western coyotes, which never were rare, moved up into Canada, bred with wolves there, and produced a larger variety of coyote, which gradually moved down into New York, appearing there in the 1920s. This variety appeared in northern New England in the 1930s and in Massachusetts in the 1950s.

Eastern coyotes average about 35 to 40 pounds in weight (western coyotes may weigh only 25 to 30 pounds). They are gray-brown in color, but occasionally their coats can be blond, red or even black. Strong swimmers, good jumpers (up to 15 feet) and swift runners (speeds of more than 30 miles per hour), eastern coyotes are also able hunters, with superior sight, smell and hearing.

Coyotes, which are mainly active at dusk and dawn, are usually no threat to humans. They are expert scavengers, eat-

Coyote

ing almost anything edible from the bottom of the food chain to the top – from berries, insects and dead animals to squirrels, birds, and, yes, even the occasional cat.

While wolves hunt in packs, eastern coyotes generally hunt alone, in mated pairs or in family groups.

Coyotes are common in the East and very adaptable in their habits, so they are slowly moving into every piece of available habitat, including cities. They often enter urban areas along riverbanks that are hidden by shrubs. They hunt mice and rats at night and then rest, perhaps in a row of hedges, during the day.

2.5 in. long

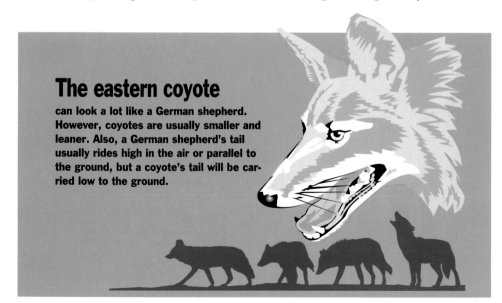

The eastern coyote

can look a lot like a German shepherd. However, coyotes are usually smaller and leaner. Also, a German shepherd's tail usually rides high in the air or parallel to the ground, but a coyote's tail will be carried low to the ground.

Beavers

Beavers are nature's engineers, creating dams and lodges that are marvels of construction.

Virtually trapped out of Massachusetts by the late 1700s, beavers have slowly moved back into all parts of the state, helped by a regulated trapping season and wildlife restoration programs.

But as the beaver population grows and spreads, these industrious animals often have to compete for space in residential areas. Having a beaver pond in the neighborhood is a delight to many people, but the ponds beavers construct by damming streams can sometimes flood back yards, roads and wells.

From their protruding, orange-tinted, buck teeth to the end of their paddlelike tails, adult beavers are usually about 3 feet long, and they can weigh 30 to 65 pounds. They use their broad, flat tails as rudders when they swim, but they also use them to warn other beavers of danger by loudly slapping them on the water's surface.

Beavers use trees as their prime building material, and they also feed on the bark. Their favorite trees include poplars, birches, maples, willows and ashes. They usually fell trees at night and are able to gnaw their way through a willow that is five inches in diameter in just a few minutes. If the mood strikes them, they will venture right into someone's back yard to claim a tree, then drag it back to their pond.

Beavers dam streams to create ponds. They spend much of their lives in water, which protects them from predators. They begin by laying branches and twigs across a stream that may be in a slight val-

Beaver

Gnawed tree

ley. Then they pack down this material with mud, extending the dam's width and height as they go.

Their trademark domed lodge usually sits near a shore of this newly-created pond. The roof of the lodge is made of twigs and mud. Inside, it has a dry platform just above the water line. There are also one or two plunge holes down into the water that provide an entrance and an exit.

Once they dam a stream, beavers typically stay in that pond five or six years, with three generations of the family often living in one lodge. In winter, they do not hibernate. They remain awake in the lodge, occasionally going out beneath the ice to feed on tree branches they've stored in the water nearby. A beaver can stay submerged in water for up to 15 minutes.

6 in. long

A beaver lodge

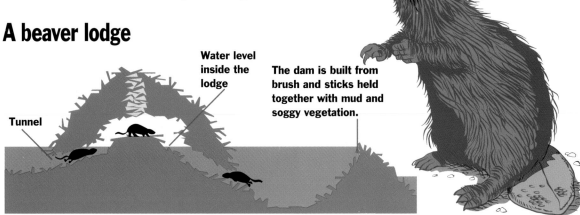

Tunnel

Water level inside the lodge

The dam is built from brush and sticks held together with mud and soggy vegetation.

Squirrels

The squirrel is one of nature's bankers, wisely putting away resources for the future. Each fall, squirrels go about collecting nuts (their favorite food) and burying them one by one for the time when the snow falls and their sources of food disappear.

When winter arrives, they can find their stores, or caches, of acorns and other nuts beneath a foot of snow, not by remembering where they buried them but by smelling them.

Squirrels are rodents, as are chipmunks, woodchucks, beavers and mice. All rodents hoard or store food to some extent.

Eastern gray squirrels are the squirrels you most commonly see in Massachusetts. With their quickness and ability to move acrobatically through the treetops, gray squirrels live easily around people and thrive wherever there are trees in urban and suburban areas.

Red squirrels are common in many areas with evergreen trees in Eastern Massachusetts, including residential neighborhoods. But northern and southern flying squirrels, which are also native to the state, are usually found in more remote forested areas.

Gray squirrels may have two litters each year, usually of two or three young per litter. One litter may be born in March or April and another in August. They nest and have their young in tree dens, which are hollow cavities in live trees. In summer, they may spend time in nests built

Eastern gray squirrel

Red squirrel

high in trees using leaves and sticks.

Although squirrels may stay in their dens for several days at a time when the weather is harsh in winter, they are active throughout the year.

Squirrels use their long bushy tails for shade, warmth, protection from rain and snow, balance when climbing and communication with other squirrels. A flying squirrel will also use its tail as a brake and rudder in flight.

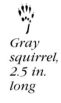

Gray squirrel, 2.5 in. long

Northern flying squirrel

Flying squirrels

don't actually fly and they don't have wings. They spread open flaps of loose skin between their front and rear legs and glide through the air.

Other mammals

Yes, there are moose and bears and deer in the woods, but it is the small critters that really populate the great outdoors.

In a square mile of good habitat, there might be a few red foxes, a few dozen striped skunks, a few hundred eastern chipmunks and a few thousand short-tailed shrews. That's not to mention the brown bats, red squirrels, gray foxes, beavers, porcupines, cottontails, weasels, coyotes, woodchucks, otters, fishers, bobcats, muskrats, hares, voles, mice, minks and moles.

But if there are that many mammals out there, why do we see so few?

Red fox

Many species are secretive and have habits that help them avoid predators (and human beings). For instance, many are nocturnal – active mainly at night. They sleep and rest in hidden places by day but then go out foraging for food once the sun goes down.

With so many animals sharing the same land, many have evolved to be specialists in where they live and what they eat so that they can survive despite the competition.

Muskrats, beavers and river otters spend much of their lives in water. Shrews, moles and voles spend much of their lives underground. Squirrels and porcupines spend much of their lives in trees. And bats fly.

Porcupines, rabbits and woodchucks, are strict vegetarians. Moles and bats eat insects. Skunks, raccoons and opossums will eat almost anything that can be eaten, including garbage.

Even among mammals, though, there are

Striped skunk

Raccoon

predators and prey, roles that are often determined by size. The shrews, mice, voles and moles tend to be the prey, while the foxes, coyotes, bobcats and fishers are often the predators.

When approached by a predator, prey animals may have specialized defenses. The opossum can act as if it's dead. The eastern cottontail can leap 15 feet. Snowshoe hares, which turn white in winter and blend with the snow, can run 30 miles per hour. Striped skunks can spray a fluid that smells terrible and can temporarily blind. Porcupines are covered with as many as 30,000 sharp quills.

In winter, many mammals either hibernate or become inactive in their dens or burrows. But some, such as coyotes, foxes, fishers and bobcats, are active throughout the year.

It is not just the deep woods and rural meadows that are home to so many mammals. Even urban and suburban neighborhoods are teeming with wild animals, and not just mammals. Many snakes, birds and insects also call this kind of habitat home.

Because many mammals, such as opossums and skunks, are nocturnal, you rarely see them in residential areas. But they're there. Ask any policeman who drives a cruiser on the midnight to dawn shift.

In fact, when an area is transformed from a rural to a residential landscape, some animals find life easier. They learn to adapt their diet to the new opportunities these neighborhoods can offer, such as bird feeders, vegetable gardens, trash cans, and healthy lawns and shrubs.

Even black bears and white-tailed deer will visit the edges of the suburbs in search of food.

Some birds that hunt, such as red-tailed hawks and great horned owls, especially like the edges of woods, which are common in residential areas. They will perch in trees on the edge of an open area and hunt mice, rabbits, squirrels and other small mammals that venture out of the woods and into the open.

Many animals, such as squirrels, chipmunks and a variety of birds, live comfortably with people and are often in sight. Other animals, including garter snakes and woodchucks, live easily among people but prefer to stay out of sight as much as possible.

Bobcat

Eastern cottontail

Porcupine

Mammals of Massachusetts

Length – Weight – Litter number and average number of young per litter – When active   – Diet – Den site – Hibernation

Bobcat 2 in. long

28 to 37 in. – 15 to 36 lbs. – One litter per year of two or three young born late April to mid-May – Active dusk to dawn in summer and also during the daytime in winter – Hunts small mammals, especially cottontails, as well as birds and snakes – Dens in a rock crevice or hollow log – Active throughout the year

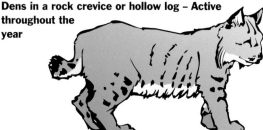

Eastern cottontail 3-4 in. long

14 to 18 in. – 2 to 4 lbs. – Three or four litters per year of three to eight young – Most active dawn to dusk – Eats mainly plant matter such as grasses and herbs in summer, and bark, twigs and buds in winter – Finds shelter year-round in brush piles, stone walls or abandoned dens and burrows – Active year-round although retreats to shelter during harsh winter weather

Porcupine 3 in. long

25 to 36 in. – 7 to 40 lbs. – One litter per year of one young born April to June – Active mainly at night – A strict vegetarian, it eats grasses, twigs, buds and bark – May spend winter in one "station tree," often a hemlock or spruce, but in harsh weather it may den in a rocky cavern or hollow log – Active throughout the year

Striped skunk 1.5 in. long

23 to 28 in. – 4 to 10 lbs. – One litter per year of five to seven young born late April to early June – Active dawn to dusk – Eats almost anything, but especially insects – Dens under a stump, in a stone wall, in an abandoned burrow or even under a house – Semi-hibernates during winter

Chipmunk 1.7 in. long

8 to 10 in. – 2 to 5 oz. – One or two litters per year of three to five young born in May and in July or August – Active all times of day – Eats mainly seeds, fruits, nuts and insects – Dens underground in a series of tunnels – Hibernates in winter but may become active for short periods

Muskrat 2.5 in. long

19 to 25 in. – 2 to 4 lbs. – Two or three litters per year of four to six young born April to July – Active mainly at night but may be seen during the day – Eats mainly aquatic plants such as cattails and water lilies – Constructs a lodge of weeds on water or digs a den in a stream bank – Active throughout the year

Opossum

 2.5 in. wide

24 to 40 in. – 9 to 13 lbs. – One or two litters per year of six to nine young born February to July – Active at night – Eats nearly anything, including insects, fruits, nuts, carrion and garbage – Dens in an abandoned burrow, tree cavity, attic, garage or building foundation – Becomes less active in winter but does not hibernate

Woodchuck

 2 in. long

16 to 32 in. – 4 to 14 lbs. – One litter per year of four or five young born early April to mid-May – Active by day, especially in the early morning and late afternoon – Eats mainly plants, such as clover and grasses – Dens in a series of underground tunnels ending in a chamber with a grass nest – Hibernates in winter

River otter

 3 in. wide

35 to 54 in. – 11 to 33 lbs. – One litter per year of two or three young born March to April – Active mainly from dusk to dawn but can be active during the day – Eats fish, frogs, turtles, snakes, and sometimes birds and small mammals – Dens in a rock crevice, under a fallen tree, in an abandoned beaver lodge or muskrat house or in thickets beside water – Active throughout the year

Red fox

 2 in. long

39 to 43 in. – 8 to 15 lbs – One litter per year of three to five young born March to April – Active mainly at dawn and dusk – Hunts small mammals and birds but also eats insects, fruits and berries – Digs its den underground with a tunnel system or may use an existing burrow – Active throughout the year

Little brown bat

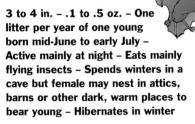

3 to 4 in. – .1 to .5 oz. – One litter per year of one young born mid-June to early July – Active mainly at night – Eats mainly flying insects – Spends winters in a cave but female may nest in attics, barns or other dark, warm places to bear young – Hibernates in winter

Raccoon

 4 in. long

23 to 38 in. – 12 to 36 lbs. – One litter per year of three or four young born late April to early May – Active at night – Eats everything from dead animals and birds to grains and garbage – Dens in a ground cavity, hollow tree, hollow log, pile of rubbish, attic or chimney – Spends winters in its den but does not hibernate

Snakes

Snakes can awaken primitive fears in us. The sudden discovery of a snake sunning itself on the front walk or slithering through the garden is enough to startle almost anyone.

But despite the impressive size of some native snakes of Massachusetts (the black rat snake can reach a length of 8 feet or more), the chance of encountering one that could truly do you harm is very small. Of the 14 species of snakes that live in the state, only two are venomous – the timber rattlesnake and the northern copperhead. And they are both endangered species in Massachusetts, found only in a few remote spots in the state, places humans rarely inhabit, such as locations high on rocky mountainsides.

Snakes live everywhere in the state, from the Berkshires to Nantucket. You're most likely to see a snake in the spring, when it is out of hibernation and basking in the sun. Snakes cannot easily adjust their body temperature in cold weather so they warm up by sunbathing.

The snake you're most likely to see is the garter snake, the most common snake in Massachusetts. Many snakes, like the

Smooth green snake

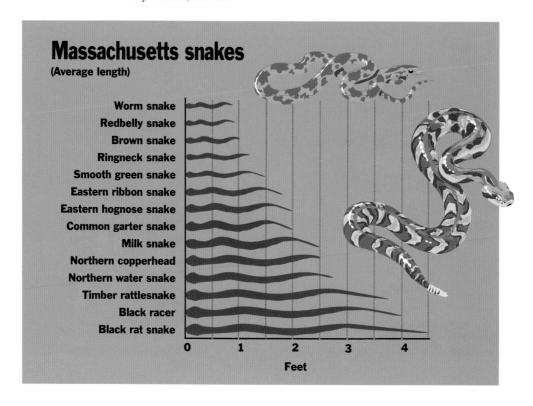

Massachusetts snakes
(Average length)

- Worm snake
- Redbelly snake
- Brown snake
- Ringneck snake
- Smooth green snake
- Eastern ribbon snake
- Eastern hognose snake
- Common garter snake
- Milk snake
- Northern copperhead
- Northern water snake
- Timber rattlesnake
- Black racer
- Black rat snake

0　1　2　3　4

Feet

Hognose snake

Garter snake

Timber rattlesnake

black racer, lay eggs, but others, like the garter snake, have live young, as many as 40 at a time.

The northern water snake is the next most common snake in the state. A harmless snake, the water snake is frequently mistaken for the poisonous water moccasin, also called the cottonmouth. However, there are no water moccasins in New England or any farther north than Virginia.

The damage from being bitten by a non-venomous snake is more psychological than physical. The wound is typically no more serious than being scratched by the thorns on a rosebush.

Larger snakes are usually more active during the day, while smaller snakes, which are more vulnerable to predators, are usually nocturnal. The larger snakes may hunt small rodents and birds. Smaller snakes usually search for insects, slugs, earthworms, frogs or toads for their meals.

Some snakes, such as the milk snake and black racer, will vibrate their tails as a display to scare predators. People often mistake this for the rattle of a timber rattlesnake. But the rattlesnake has a very distinct rattle on it that when shaken sounds almost like a baby's rattle.

In winter, snakes in Massachusetts hibernate in burrows or hollows or even in holes in the foundations of homes.

Most snakes are hatched or born in the summer, and they are left on their own to find food from the start. As snakes grow, they periodically shed their outer skin – like throwing away an old set of clothes – because they outgrow it. This is called shedding, or molting.

Milk snake

Ringneck snake

Turtles

Even nature believes you don't fix what isn't broken. Despite being slower and more awkward than almost any other animal, turtles have changed remarkably little since they first appeared nearly 200 million years ago, during the age of the dinosaurs,.

Their basic design – everything contained inside a hard shell – has worked very well for them, providing them excellent protection against predators. In fact, turtles may live longer than any other species of animal. Some sea turtles live nearly 150 years, twice as long as most humans. Even common painted turtles can live up to 50 years.

The chief threat to turtles is humans. Many turtles are disappearing from the wild because they are collected for the pet trade. Some species are vanishing because their nesting sites, the places where they go to lay eggs, have been developed for businesses and homes.

Like snakes, turtles are reptiles, which means they cannot warm their bodies from the inside the way humans and

Box turtle, 4 to 8.5 in.

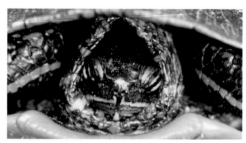

Painted turtle

Turtles all lay eggs in the ground. Even turtles that spend nearly all their lives in water come onto land to bury up to several dozen eggs in shallow holes they dig in early summer. Most turtle eggs hatch in early September.

other mammals do. Instead, reptiles must take action to warm up. For instance, they can bask in the sun. And on cool spring days or on summer mornings, you will often see turtles in ponds doing just this, as they sit on top of logs or rocks.

Turtles have no teeth. They use their hard bills to scissor apart their food. They eat insects, worms, fish and some plants.

A turtle's shell is both its mobile home and its protection. The top part of the shell, called the carapace, is attached to the turtle's rib cage and backbone. The lower half of the shell is called the plastron. Despite what you see in cartoons, turtles cannot leave their shells.

Turtles have lungs but no gills. Some are able to breathe underwater by absorbing oxygen from the water through their exposed skin.

In winter, most turtles settle down into the mud at the bottom of ponds or rivers to hibernate. Land turtles, such as the box turtle, dig beneath soft dirt or decaying leaves to hibernate.

Worldwide, there are nearly 250 species of turtles, including about a dozen that can be found in Massachusetts. The most common turtle found in the state is the painted turtle. It lives almost anywhere there are ponds, lakes or slow-moving streams or rivers.

Snapping turtles, which spend most of their time underwater, are the next most common species, but they are rarely seen except during the breeding season. Like all turtles, they come onto land to lay their eggs.

The largest snapping turtle ever found, 76 pounds, was caught in Massachusetts.

Snapping turtle, 8 to 19 in.

Spotted turtle, 3.5 to 5 in.

Painted turtle, 4 to 10 in.

Musk turtle (stinkpot), 3 to 5.5 in.

59

Frogs

If there were an animal Olympics, frogs would certainly be competitors in the standing long jump. Some can leap 10 times their body length.

Lots of animals are specialists physically. They have a feature that gives them an advantage over other animals in finding food or defending themselves, and that's why their species has survived over the centuries. Frogs use their tremendous jumping ability both to escape predators and to pounce on a meal.

Frogs are amphibians, which means they spend part of their lives in water and part on land. They are also among the animals that undergo metamorphosis, which means a "change in form." As young tadpoles (also called polliwogs), they live in water and look like small fish with large rounded heads. They have gills, tails and no legs. But eventually they will develop lungs and legs, they will lose their tails, and, as frogs, they will be able to live on land.

There are more than 3,500 species of frogs worldwide. Nearly a dozen species can be found in Massachusetts.

Most adult frogs have large hind legs for jumping, hind toes that are connected by webbing, no claws and tiny teeth (if they have any at all).

Some, such as the eastern spadefoot, are rare enough in the state that you will

Bullfrog, 3 to 8 in.

probably never come across one in your lifetime. But others, like bullfrogs and green frogs, are so common, you can't miss them. In spring or summer, walk down to the edge of any pond and you may see a green frog sitting very still on the bank or a bullfrog peering at you from the water, its two bulging eyes and a bit of its head breaking the pond's surface.

Spend any time around a pond and you'll also hear frogs calling, or chorusing, especially during breeding season, which usually peaks in April and May. Male frogs are the ones making all the noise. They call to attract females and to announce that a certain territory is theirs.

A frog enhances its call by using a loose pouch of skin at its throat that it can fill

Green frog, 2 to 4 in.

Spring peeper, .75 to 1.5 in.

with air. When it calls, the sound that is produced in its larynx enters this air-filled chamber and reverberates, like an echo in a cave, becoming even more intense. A male frog might repeat its call thousands of times in one night.

Frogs all lay jellylike eggs in water, often thousands of eggs at a time, which eventually hatch to become tadpoles.

In winter, frogs become inactive, settling down into the mud at the bottom of ponds or taking refuge under piles of dead leaves or in underground tunnels on land. In the coldest weather, some even partially freeze but are still able to thaw out and resume their lives in the spring.

Most frogs eat insects, such as ants and flies, as well as worms and snails. However, the bullfrog, which is the largest native Massachusetts frog, will eat fish, snakes, mice and even small birds or newly-hatched turtles that venture too close.

Humans versus animals

Human world record as of August 1998 compared to the observed performance of animals in the wild

Marathon

(26 miles, 385 yards)
Human: 2 hr., 6 min., 50 sec.
Pronghorn antelope: About 45 min.

High jump

Human: 8 ft., .5 in.
Killer whale: About 19 ft., 6 in.

Speed on land

(100 meter dash)
Human: 9.84 sec.
Cheetah: About 3.6 sec.

Speed in water

(100 meter freestyle)
Human: 48.21 sec.
Sailfish: About 3.3 sec.

Long jump

Human: 29 ft., 4.5 in.
Snow leopard: About 60 ft.

Problems with amphibians

In Minnesota in 1995, a middle school class studying frogs in a farm pond made a startling discovery. Nearly half the leopard frogs they found that day were deformed. Some had missing legs while others had extra legs.

Since then, similar discoveries about both frogs and salamanders have been made in other places around the United States.

In addition, populations of frogs in many places in the world are declining dramatically. What makes the problem more mysterious is that the disappearances often occur in remote rural areas, such as Yosemite National Park in California. Yet in many urban areas, such as those around many eastern U.S. cities, populations of frogs and other amphibians are stable, and the rate of deformities is no higher than what would occur naturally in the wild.

Researchers do not know the reason for the troubling changes. It could be the effect of increased ultraviolet radiation from the sun on the development of amphibians' delicate eggs, a problem created by the thinning of the atmosphere's ozone layer. It could also be a fungus, chemical pesticides in the water, or a number of other causes.

A recent five-year study of frogs, salamanders, snakes and turtles in Massachusetts found that they do not seem to be disappearing from their historic habitats. However, in areas where a species' favorite habitat is declining, such as ponds, the population of that species is declining.

Frog or toad?

● You can usually tell the two apart by the texture of their skins. Frogs tend to have smoother skin, and they spend a lot of time in and around water. Toads have rougher, warty skin and usually can be found on land. Technically, though, a toad is a kind of frog.

Leopard frog, 2 to 5 in.

Gray treefrog, 1 to 2.5 in.

American toad, 2 to 4.5 in.

Vernal pools

On the first warm night that follows a heavy rain each spring, an amazing event occurs. Certain frogs and salamanders that are rarely seen at any other time of the year come out of hiding and begin moving through the woods in great numbers.

Crowds of frogs. Parades of salamanders.

They are migrating to pools of water left by melted snow on forest floors. They may cross roads, hike up hills and climb over rocks and fallen trees in their determination to reach these temporary patches of water, called vernal pools.

Because the water dries up in the heat of summer, these pools do not contain fish. And that makes them ideal breeding ponds for these amphibians. There will be no predatory fish in the water to eat their eggs or their developing young.

In Massachusetts, wood frogs make this trek, as do spotted, blue-spotted and Jefferson salamanders.

From early March to mid-April, you can locate these breeding pools by the sounds that come from them at night. Wood frogs will chorus, making a noise that resembles ducks quacking.

Once these amphibians reach their vernal pool, which they may return to year after year, they must court, breed and lay their eggs in a short period of time.

They are active by day, but most of the activity is at night, especially among the

Spotted salamander, 6 to 10 in.

salamanders.

If you can locate a vernal pool in the spring, take a flashlight, shine it on the water after dark, and you might see dozens of these creatures swimming here and there.

Wood frog, 1.5 to 3.5 in.

Butterflies

What monarch butterflies do each fall is just about the definition of impossible.

Each September tens of millions of these regal orange and black butterflies leave their summer breeding grounds in the eastern United States and Canada and flutter off toward their winter home on a few remote mountainsides in Central Mexico. They return to the very same spots, the very same trees, that previous generations returned to in their southern migrations for hundreds, maybe even thousands of years. Then, in the spring, they lift off nearly all at once, forming great clouds of butterflies that fill the sky as they return north.

But the astounding thing is that adult monarchs may live less than one month. That means that none of the monarchs that leave Mexico in the spring will be among those that return in the fall. Instead, it is their great-great-grandchildren that will somehow find their way back to those few Mexican mountainsides with no one in their band of migrating monarchs ever having been there.

Monarch

How do they do it? Is it in their genes? Are they guided by the earth's magnetic field? Or is it just one of the mysteries of animal instincts?

Butterflies, like all insects, go through a metamorphosis, or a change in appearance, except that for butterflies it is one of the most striking changes. Butterflies have four stages to their lives – egg, larva (also called a caterpillar), pupa (also called a chrysalis), then adult butterfly.

Banded hairstreak

The pupa, which is a shell-like covering that forms from the caterpillar, hangs by thin threads from a twig or leaf. Inside, the caterpillar can change from a fairly clumsy, slow-moving and perhaps even ugly creature into what can be a beautiful, brilliantly colored butterfly, carrying the colors of the rainbow on its fragile wings.

Butterflies feed on nectar, a sweet liquid found deep inside flowers. To do this, a butterfly uses its proboscis, a long narrow tube, like a drinking straw, that can be almost as long as its body. When not in use, the proboscis is kept curled up where you would expect the butterfly's mouth to be.

Butterflies need the heat of the sun to warm their bodies, so you will usually see them flying only during the middle of the day. At night, they rest and conserve energy.

Butterflies have three body parts, six legs, and four wings – a pair each of front and back wings.

The colors on their wings are created by tiny scales of many different hues that fit together like tiles in a mosaic.

Adult butterflies usually live only a few days or weeks, surviving mainly to mate and produce

Butterfly or moth?

● There are lots of differences. Butterflies usually fly during the day. Moths usually fly at night.

Butterflies tend to rest with their wings folded up over their heads or stretched flat to each side. Moths often lay their wings flat and behind them while resting.

The antennae of butterflies are thin and end in a knob. Those of moths do not end in a knob and are often feathery.

Butterflies usually have bolder and brighter colors than moths.

eggs. The female searches for certain kinds of plants on which to lay her eggs, since they are food plants for the young caterpillars. Monarchs choose milkweed. White admirals like wild cherry and poplar leaves. Tiger swallowtails prefer black cherry leaves.

There are about 100 species of butterflies that breed in Massachusetts. About 30 other species have been seen occasionally in the state.

Flight times for Massachusetts butterflies

(I = first generation, II = second generation, III = third generation)

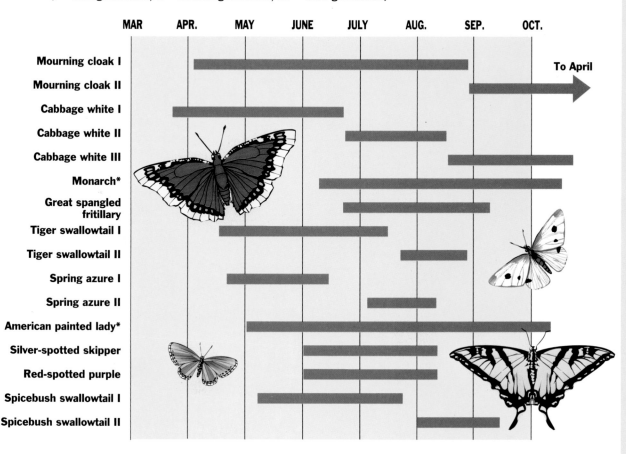

* Three generations are mixed together through the season

Mourning cloak – 3 to 3.5 in. – One of the earliest butterflies to appear in the spring, the mourning cloak also overwinters as an adult in New England.

Monarch – 3.5 to 4 in. – Monarchs are among the butterflies that migrate north in spring and south in the fall, just like many birds.

Eastern tiger swallowtail – 3 to 5 in.– One of the most common butterflies in Massachusetts, it's eggs are often laid on the leaves of black cherry trees.

Spicebush swallowtail – 3.5 to 4.5 in. – This swallowtail feeds on the nectar of milkweed and Joe-pye weed. It likes forest openings and meadows.

Eastern black swallowtail – 2.5 to 3.5 in. – Black swallowtails are attracted to carrot or parsnip plants growing in gardens.

Red-spotted purple – 3 to 3.5 in. – This butterfly feeds on the leaves of willows, poplars and aspens and is often seen in forest openings and meadows.

The measurement given is each butterfly's typical wingspan.

Spring azure – About 1 in. – One of the first butterflies to appear in the spring, the spring azure is often spotted in woodland openings.

Cabbage white – 1.5 to 2 in. – Perhaps the butterfly most often seen because of its white color, the cabbage white prefers fields and gardens.

Clouded sulphur – 1.5 to 2 in. – This butterfly can be seen in any open area, such as a field or garden. It especially likes clover patches.

Pearl crescent – 1 to 1.5 in. – A common butterfly of fields and meadows, the pearl crescent, in the larva stage, often feeds on native asters.

Eastern comma – 1.5 to 2 in. – The comma is one of the butterflies that remains in the region during winter, hibernating in protected places until spring.

American copper – About 1 in. – A butterfly of fields and meadows, the American copper tends to have its brightest colors early in the spring.

Common ringlet – 1 to 2 in. – This grass feeder has spread from Canada south into the U.S. Northeast and now occupies all of New England.

Little wood satyr – 1.5 to 2 in. – Often seen at the edges of woods and in meadows, this butterfly feeds primarily on woodland grasses.

Banded hairstreak – 1 to 1.5 in. – This hairstreak prefers sunlit woodland edges and clearings. It is often seen on milkweed plants and daisies.

Silver-spotted skipper – 1.5 to 2.5 in. – Found throughout North America, this skipper is often seen in grassy open areas and in gardens.

Great spangled fritillary – 2.5 to 3 in. – A swift flyer, this fritillary will stop to feed on the nectar of violets, clover and black-eyed Susans.

Baltimore checkerspot – About 2 in. – The Baltimore, which prefers meadows, has a checkerboard pattern on the underside of its wings.

Sudbury River, Great Meadows National Wildlife Refuge, Concord

Metamorphosis

At most family reunions, get everyone together in one room and you can usually see a resemblance.

But put a caterpillar and a butterfly side by side, or a tadpole and a frog next to each other, and not only is there no family resemblance, there's not even a species resemblance.

Nature devised this dramatic change in appearance, this metamorphosis, as a way of ensuring that these species would survive.

Why does it happen?

Many features of plants and animals – the long legs of a great blue heron, the rich color of a rose, the sharp beak of a hawk – evolved or developed because they give a species a better chance for survival. They are features that give it an edge in finding food or in reproducing or in protecting itself from predators.

Metamorphosis is no different. Species that change form (and all amphibians and insects go through some type of metamorphosis) can occupy two very different places in the ecosystem. The young may

Bullfrog, top, and green frog

eat one kind of food, go through metamorphosis, and then eat a different kind of food as adults. That means there is more food available for the entire species, increasing its chance for survival.

Tadpoles are vegetarians, but adult bull-

Monarch metamorphosis

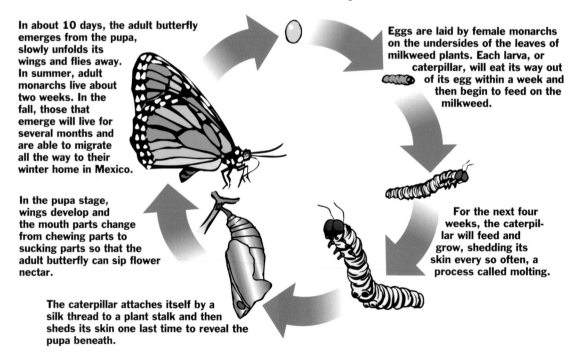

In about 10 days, the adult butterfly emerges from the pupa, slowly unfolds its wings and flies away. In summer, adult monarchs live about two weeks. In the fall, those that emerge will live for several months and are able to migrate all the way to their winter home in Mexico.

In the pupa stage, wings develop and the mouth parts change from chewing parts to sucking parts so that the adult butterfly can sip flower nectar.

The caterpillar attaches itself by a silk thread to a plant stalk and then sheds its skin one last time to reveal the pupa beneath.

Eggs are laid by female monarchs on the undersides of the leaves of milkweed plants. Each larva, or caterpillar, will eat its way out of its egg within a week and then begin to feed on the milkweed.

For the next four weeks, the caterpillar will feed and grow, shedding its skin every so often, a process called molting.

Monarch pupae

Monarch caterpillar

frogs eat almost anything, from plants to small birds.

Most caterpillars are also vegetarians. But adult butterflies sip the rich nectar they find in flowers.

Having different forms at different stages of life can help in other ways as well.

Caterpillars do almost nothing but eat and grow, and they are well-designed to do just that. They are able to avoid predators to some extent because most can blend into vegetation. They are also able to blend into their environment as pupae, the stage in which they are surrounded by mummylike coverings and undergo the changes that make them adult butterflies. Then, in the butterfly stage, they can fly to new areas to lay eggs and spread their species.

The changes tadpoles and caterpillars go through during metamorphosis are striking. Bullfrog tadpoles, which will be going from a life spent entirely in water to a life on land and in water, have to develop lungs during the change. Also, their tails have to be reabsorbed into their bodies, their limbs have to develop fully, and their jaws have to change, since they will be eating new and different foods.

Caterpillars, during the pupa stage, have to lose their many legs as well as develop wings and sex organs. Their mouth parts also have to change from chewing parts to sucking parts so that they will be able to feed on flower nectar.

For frogs, the metamorphosis usually lasts from several days to a few weeks. For butterflies, it may last from a few days to several months.

Bullfrog metamorphosis

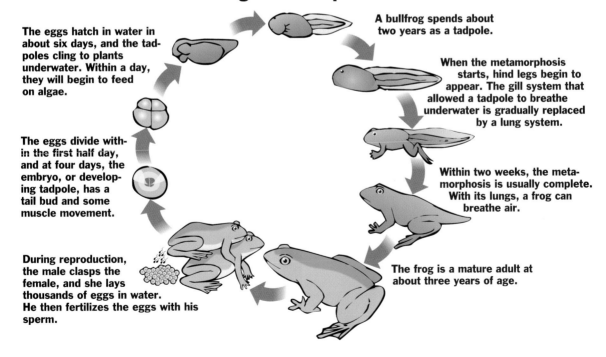

The eggs hatch in water in about six days, and the tadpoles cling to plants underwater. Within a day, they will begin to feed on algae.

The eggs divide within the first half day, and at four days, the embryo, or developing tadpole, has a tail bud and some muscle movement.

During reproduction, the male clasps the female, and she lays thousands of eggs in water. He then fertilizes the eggs with his sperm.

A bullfrog spends about two years as a tadpole.

When the metamorphosis starts, hind legs begin to appear. The gill system that allowed a tadpole to breathe underwater is gradually replaced by a lung system.

Within two weeks, the metamorphosis is usually complete. With its lungs, a frog can breathe air.

The frog is a mature adult at about three years of age.

Spiders

What tangled webs they weave. Worldwide, there are more than 30,000 kinds of spiders. About 700 varieties can be found in New England.

You can tell a spider by its two body sections and eight legs. Most also have eight eyes. Spiders are generally active only at night, and they are not very aggressive. Even those with the strongest venom will attack humans only as a defensive measure, preferring to retreat from battle whenever possible.

Because of New England's chilly winters, most spiders found in this region live just one season, hatching in the spring, breeding and laying eggs in the summer, and dying in the fall.

But a certain number manage to live through the winter. And they may try to escape the elements by seeking refuge in the cozy interior of your home or apartment. A large house can be home to hundreds of spiders in winter, with the human residents barely aware of their presence.

Most spiders you are likely to encounter in Massachusetts would be too small to pose a threat. As a general rule, only those with a body over half an inch in length (not including legs) have fangs capable of penetrating human skin. But that does not mean they are dangerous. Even larger spiders that bite are not usually a serious danger.

Just about all spiders are venomous. Even the smaller ones use venom to weaken or kill their prey. But only a few spiders have strong enough venom to cause harm to a human being.

Shamrock spider, .7 in. (The body lengths are given for the females, which are usually larger than the males.)

Black-and-yellow garden spider, 1 in.

The two most venomous spiders to be found in the United States are the brown recluse and the black widow. The brown recluse may occasionally appear in Massachusetts as a hitchhiker on furniture or clothes brought from areas where it is native, such as the South. The black widow is also rare in the state but is occasionally reported on Cape Cod and the islands – Nantucket and Martha's Vineyard. The female is black, with a red marking on its abdomen that is shaped like an hourglass.

The female black widow earned her name because soon after mating she eats the male. The males of most species of spiders are not treated so badly.

The largest spider someone in Massachusetts might commonly cross paths with is the wolf spider, a resident in winter of dark cellars and attics. Its body can be more than an inch long.

Daddy-long-legs, .4 in., (not a true spider)

Wolf spider, 1 in.

Spider webs

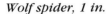

The delicate webs that decorate dew-covered meadows or that float weightlessly in the corners of attic ceilings are actually miracles of engineering. Pound for pound, the silk in a spider web is stronger than steel.

Silk is produced in a spider's abdomen, starting out as a sticky gel created in silk glands. It turns into a solid as it is pushed out of the body. The final strand of silk may be less than a tenth the thickness of a human hair. Yet it can hold an astounding amount of weight. As a comparison, a one-inch thick rope would have to hold up 15 automobiles to have the same strength as some spider silk.

Aside from creating webs with their silk to snare passing flies and other prey, spiders use it as a safety line so that they can drop down from ceilings or branches. They also use silk to wrap their eggs for protection and to wrap prey for a later meal. A spider may produce up to eight different kinds of silk, each for a different use.

Spider web

Insects

What they lack in size they make up for in numbers. More than a million species of insects have been identified in the world, nearly four times as many species as all other animals. And that may be only a small fraction of all the insect species that actually exist.

Despite their small size and short lives (some aphids are lucky to live ten days), insects are highly successful creatures. They have been able to thrive in almost every kind of habitat in almost every region of the world.

In fact, their short lives help to make them so successful. Insects reproduce quickly and in great numbers. So if there is any change in their surroundings – for instance, if the temperature warms dramatically – the chances are good that they will produce some young from the thousands of eggs they might lay (some termites lay 2,000 eggs a day) that have the right combination of genes to overcome the warmer weather. Some of those young will survive, reproduce more young with similar genes, and soon the local population will have adapted to the warmer climate and be thriving again.

Species that take a relatively long time to reproduce, such as some birds, which may have just two or three young a season, would not be able to adapt to dramat-

Bumble bee, .7 in.

ic changes in their habitat so quickly. Such changes might completely wipe out their local population.

All insects have certain things in common. They have six legs, three body sections and antennae. Spiders, with their eight legs, are not true insects.

Yes, most insects can hear, taste, touch, smell and see, but many of them do these things in very different ways than humans. Crickets hear with their knees. Flies taste with their feet. And some moths and beetles smell with their antennae.

Most insects have two main eyes and two or three smaller, simpler eyes. The

Cecropia caterpillar, 4 in.

Praying mantis, 2.5 in.

Honey bee, .5 in.

True katydid, 2 in.

Northern bluet, a damselfly, 1.5 in.

Twelve-spotted skimmer, a dragonfly, 2 in.

main eyes are sometimes made up of thousands of individual lenses that each produce an image.

Human eyes have one lens each, so the human brain has to interpret only the two images that its eyes send it. But a dragonfly's eyes may have 28,000 lenses each, which means its tiny brain has to interpret that many images in order to understand what it is seeing.

Every insect goes through metamorphosis, a change in appearance that marks a new stage of its life. Most insects look completely different as adults than as young emerging from eggs. Many are flightless when young but have wings as adults.

If you think the wings of a hummingbird move fast, one species of midge, a tiny insect also known as a "no-see-um," beats its wings almost 1,000 times a second. That's nearly 13 times faster than a hummingbird beats its wings.

When storm systems sweep up the Atlantic Coast, they often carry with them insects plucked from other coastal regions. So Cape Cod, the Massachusetts islands and other coastal areas in the state are often visited by insects you would normally see only in the Carolinas, Maryland, Delaware and other coastal states farther south.

Insects of Massachusetts

House flies

Unwelcome guests at a picnic and a noisy distraction when they get inside a home or apartment, house flies have short lives and reproduce quickly. Their eggs can hatch in just 10 to 24 hours, and the larvae can grow to adulthood in 10 days. A house fly may be hatched, mature, reproduce and die in the space of just four or five weeks, which means several generations of house flies can occur during one summer.

These flies do not bite, but they can spread disease. They may pick up harmful bacteria by landing on garbage, and then land on food someone is about to eat.

Mosquitoes

It is only the female mosquito that will bite you. The males feed mainly on flower nectar. The females, which need a meal of blood before laying eggs, choose a potential victim by sensing certain chemicals, such as the carbon dioxide that mammals exhale, and by detecting body heat.

Mosquitoes are most active at dawn, dusk and at night. They hatch from eggs laid in still pools of water such as rainwater that collects in roadside ditches or in discarded tires.

June bugs

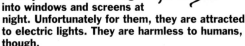

Also called May beetles, June bugs are often seen buzzing around porch lights, or they are heard crashing into windows and screens at night. Unfortunately for them, they are attracted to electric lights. They are harmless to humans, though.

As adults, they feed on the leaves of many common trees.

Dragonflies and damselflies

Dragonflies, also known as darning needles, and damselflies dine mainly on mosquitoes. That's why you usually see them hovering and darting about in the air over ponds and other water bodies. They do not bite humans. You can tell a dragonfly from a damselfly by how it holds its wings when at rest. A dragonfly will stretch them out from side to side.

Damselflies rest with their wings folded in back of them close to their sides. Both dragonflies and damselflies mate in midair.

Ants

Like bees and other social insects, ants live in organized societies, where the members work together to keep the colony functioning.

In all ant colonies, one queen ant is responsible for laying the eggs and producing the young.

Black carpenter ants, which are about a half-inch long, build their nests in dead wood, creating a series of tunnels and rooms. Unlike termites, they do not eat wood. They only tunnel into it. Little black ants, which may be one-fourth the size of carpenter ants, usually build their nest underground, forming a little mound at the opening.

Bee or wasp?

● Both can sting if bothered, but bees tend to have hairy bodies while wasps usually do not. Also, many bees, such as bumble bees and honey bees, have on their hind legs "pollen baskets" made of stiff hairs, where they carry the pollen they collect on their visits to flowers. Hornets and yellow jackets are kinds of wasps.

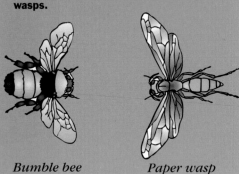

Bumble bee   *Paper wasp*

Honey bees

Honey bees live in ordered societies, where each bee has a job. A honey bee hive may have 50,000 members. There is only one queen bee, and her job is to lay the eggs and produce the young. There may be 1,000 male drones in the hive, and their only job is to mate with the queen, although only one will be successful. The rest of the hive's members are female worker bees, and they can have many jobs during their brief lives.

DAY 24-28
The worker bee's first job is as a cleaner, tidying up the hive.

DAY 28-36
It becomes a nurse, caring for the larvae.

DAY 3-24
The larva emerges from the egg and grows to adulthood as a worker bee.

DAY 36-50
It becomes a builder, adding to the hive, or a soldier, guarding the hive's entrance.

DAY 1-3
The egg is laid and develops.

DAY 50-70
It becomes a food collector, searching outside the hive for nectar and pollen until the day it dies.

At other times, a worker honey bee may be a fanner, beating its wings to keep the hive cool, or an undertaker, removing the bodies of dead bees from the hive.

Ladybugs

Probably the best known of beetles, ladybugs (also known as ladybird beetles) are among the most valuable beetles to humans as well. They generally do not eat plants, but they do eat small insects that eat plants, which makes them valuable to farmers. In this region, you might see ladybugs with two, nine or 13 spots.

Fireflies

Also called lightning bugs, these beetles produce light in the tips of their abdomens by combining chemicals they produce and store in their bodies.

Their blinking in summer is part of their mating process. Males fly about, flashing their lights, while females sit on leaves and branches. By the pattern of the flashing, a female knows if a male is of her species. If he is, she may answer with flashes of her own to invite him to her.

Grasshoppers and crickets

The "songs" of grasshoppers, like those of crickets, are the music of summer nights. However, these insects don't sing the way humans do. Grasshoppers rub rough parts of their wings together to create their music, and crickets rub their wings together.

Pond life

Nothing seems so alive as a pond in summer. A small pond just a few dozen feet across can seem to support more species of wildlife than a whole forest – frogs, birds, turtles, fish, insects and wildflowers all crowding in together, like people at a community swimming pool in August.

In fact, ponds are communities, and like most communities, they have distinct neighborhoods. There are some species that prefer the shore edges, while others like deeper water. Some stay on the water's surface, and others rarely leave the pond's bottom.

For a plant, one neighborhood may provide a better combination of sunlight and nutrients than another. For an animal, a certain neighborhood may increase its chances of survival because it offers more food and protection from predators than another neighborhood.

Freshwater ponds tend to be home to many of the same plant and animal species, no matter where you go in the region. You might see wildflowers such as

Mallards

blue flag irises on the shores, pickerel-weed in the shallow water and fragrant water lilies floating in deeper water. You might see mallards paddling across the water or a kingfisher perched in the trees, ready to dive into the water to catch a passing tadpole.

In the water, there will probably be frogs – bullfrogs and green frogs – as well as fish – pumpkinseeds and bullheads. And all around a pond, there are insects –

Lily pads

dragonflies, mayflies, water striders and, yes, pesky mosquitoes, which get eaten by the dragonflies.

Life in a pond follows a seasonal clock. In January, a pond is mostly asleep. Only a few animals stir under the thick ice that covers it – perhaps a muskrat feeding on the remains of water plants or a yellow perch slowly gliding along.

By March, with the sun higher in the sky, the ice around the pond edges may be turning to slush. Red-winged blackbird males return to establish nesting territories around the pond. The eggs of insects, such as midges, hatch in the mud along the shore, and water lilies are growing new shoots. Finally, the ice melts completely.

In April, the shallows of the pond are crowded with developing insects. Turtles bask on logs and rocks to warm up. In May, leaves appear on trees around the pond, and mallards are building their nests around the pond edges and laying eggs. Damselflies hover over the water.

By June, the pond has come fully to life. Mayflies are hatching in great numbers. The young of red-winged blackbirds are being born. The chorusing of bullfrogs and green frogs can be heard at night.

In July, microscopic life in the water becomes thick. Mallards and their young feed on submerged plants. Muskrats feed on plants in the shallows. There is motion everywhere in and around the pond.

In August, things grow quieter. The task of reproduction for most pond wildlife is complete, so their main job of the summer is over. The water may turn green from algae growth. And the heads of frogs sit motionless above the water, like tiny islands.

In September and October, many birds abandon the pond to fly south for the winter. At the first frost, leaves on many pond plants turn brown and start to die. Water lilies may break off from their roots and float to shore, pushed by chilly autumn gusts.

As the days grow shorter and colder, frogs and turtles spend more of their day at the bottom of the pond, where temperatures are warmer.

Eventually, ice begins to form along the pond edges. It will gradually grow thicker, working its way to the center until, once again, the pond is frozen over, waiting for spring, when its cycle of life will begin again.

Pond neighborhoods
Here are some of the wildlife species that can be found in different neighborhoods of a pond in summer.

Air
Kingfisher, dragonfly, damselfly, mosquito, little brown bat, mayfly

Shore
Bullfrog and green frog basking, blue flag, raccoon, purple loosestrife, weeping willow, green ash, painted turtle, red-backed salamander

Shallow water
Green heron, great blue heron, bluegill, pickerelweed, cattail, water snake, duckweed, arrowhead, muskrat

Water surface
Whirligig beetle, water strider, springtail, water lily, mallard, bullfrog, green frog

Deeper water
Yellow perch, beaver

Pond bottom
Snapping turtle, bullhead, aquatic earthworm, crayfish, dragonfly nymph

Ocean life

The oceans were home to living things well before the land was. And just as land animals have evolved to take forms that increase their species' chance of survival, so have marine creatures.

Finding food and trying not to be something else's food are two of the main reasons why different forms of life have the different forms they do. To be fast on land so that you can escape predators or so that you can be a predator yourself, you need strong legs and a sleek runner's body, like an antelope or a cheetah. If you're not going to be a fast runner, you need something else that protects you, like the tough outer shell of a turtle. You can also be well protected if you have the huge size of an elephant or the small size of a spider, which can hide from predators in tiny openings.

In the water, the same rules hold true. A marine creature survives best if it has speed or a protective physical feature.

To be fast swimmers, many marine animals, such as sharks and dolphins, have smooth, torpedo-shaped bodies so that they can cut easily through the water. Many of the slow movers, such as clams, lobsters and horseshoe crabs, have a hard outer shell. Summer flounders have camouflage. They are flat fish that lie on the ocean bottom, settling into the sand and changing their color to match their surroundings.

The huge size of whales makes them safe

Horseshoe crab

from most marine predators. And the four-spine stickleback – a very small fish, only about two inches in length – stays close to underwater vegetation near shorelines, where it can hide from larger predatory fish that come near.

Starfish have a unique way to increase their chances of survival. A predator may take a bite out of a starfish, but even if it loses four of its five arms and most of its central disk, a starfish can still regrow its entire body.

Just as any kid knows it's fun to play in the ocean, dolphins, porpoises and seals have apparently learned the same thing. Dolphins will often ride in the waves created by moving ships, much like body surfers at the beach.

Several decades ago, harbor and gray seals were rare sights in Massachusetts waters. They would often steal fish from fishermen's nets, so bounties were offered for dead seals. That practice was ended in

Harbor seal

1964, and in 1972 the federal Marine Mammal Protection Act was passed, offering further protection. Now, thousands of seals gather in winter on the Massachusetts coast, basking in the sun on Calf Island in Boston Harbor, off Chatham, on Monomoy Island and on Salisbury Beach, as well as in other locations.

As a result of overfishing, many species of fish are no longer as plentiful in Massachusetts coastal waters as they once were. However, many kinds of shellfish – the creatures that produce seashells – are flourishing.

Because Cape Cod can be the dividing line for the warm currents flowing up from the south and colder currents flowing down from the north, you will find certain shells more often north of the Cape and others more often south of it. Mussels prefer colder water, while more whelks, scallops and quahogs can usually be found in the warmer water of shallow bays in Southeastern Massachusetts.

Seashells by the seashore

Blue mussel
1 to 4 in. – Mussels often form great colonies, attaching to rocks, shells, wood pilings or other solid structures near or below the low-tide mark.

Atlantic bay scallop
1.5 to 4 in. – These scallops normally live in the shallow water of protected bays where sea grasses grow.

Eastern oyster
2 to 8 in. – Oysters are usually found below the low-tide line. They are often found in clusters.

Common periwinkle
1 in. or less – Periwinkles often attach to rocks or vegetation in the zone between low and high tide where they feed on algae.

Northern quahog
2.5 to 5 in. – Also called hard-shelled clams, quahogs usually live in sand or mud in protected bays and inlets.

Knobbed whelk
4 to 9 in. – These marine snails feed on clams. They are typically found in sand in shallow water.

Channeled whelk
3 to 8 in. – Whelks are sea snails, and channeled whelks are found from Cape Cod to Florida on sandy or muddy ocean bottoms.

Soft-shelled clam
1 to 5 in. – These shellfish, also known as steamer clams, are usually found in sand or mud.

Fish

Pumpkinseed – 6 to 9 in., typical length for adults – fresh water

White perch – 8 to 10 in. – fresh and salt water

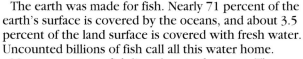

Rainbow trout – 16 to 22 in. – fresh and salt water

Striped bass – 24 to 36 in. – fresh and salt water

The earth was made for fish. Nearly 71 percent of the earth's surface is covered by the oceans, and about 3.5 percent of the land surface is covered with fresh water. Uncounted billions of fish call all this water home.

Most ocean-going fish live close to the coast. The oceans, which have an average depth of three miles, are shallower near coasts, and more of the foods fish prefer can be found in shallow waters than in deep waters.

A coastal region, Eastern Massachusetts is rich in habitats that fish populate. It has freshwater habitats, such as rivers, ponds, lakes and streams. With all its islands and bays, it has more than 1,200 miles of coastline where the salt water of the ocean meets the land. And it has estuaries, semi-enclosed places on the coast where streams and rivers flow into the ocean and fresh water and salt water mix. The mouths of the Westport and Merrimack rivers are rich estuaries, as are Waquoit Bay, Wellfleet Harbor and Plymouth-Kingston-Duxbury Bay.

Some fish, such as the yellow perch and the pumpkinseed, are found only in freshwater habitats. You will find the halibut and great white shark only in the salt water of the ocean. However, the striped killifish and the mummichog spend most of their time in the mixed waters of estuaries.

Some fish split their time between fresh water and salt water. Atlantic salmon and sea lampreys are hatched from eggs laid in freshwater rivers and streams, but they spend most of their lives in the Atlantic Ocean before returning upriver to spawn, or produce eggs. The American eel does just the opposite, laying its eggs in salt water but living mostly in fresh water.

Fish breathe underwater by drawing oxygen from water as it passes over their gills. Sharks are fish, but dolphins, porpoises and other whales are mammals that breathe air into their lungs like human beings, holding their breath when they submerge. (Some whales can stay submerged for more than an hour on one breath.)

All living things have to reproduce to make sure there will be future generations of their species. But different creatures have different reproductive strategies. Some animals are protective parents and stay with their young as they grow (human beings and most birds). Others lay eggs or give birth and then let the young take care of themselves (fish and frogs.)

The animals that feed and protect their young usually have to produce only a few young each season to guarantee that the species will continue. Their care increases the chances that the young will survive into adulthood so that they can reproduce. But animals that do not care for their young usually have to produce hundreds, thousands or even millions of eggs or young each season to guarantee that enough will survive to reproductive age to ensure that the species can continue. A female bluefin tuna may produce 25 million eggs in a single season.

Fishing was one of the first real industries for European settlers arriving in Massachusetts. The coastal waters were rich in finfish and shellfish, from striped bass and haddock to lobsters and clams. But overfishing through the centuries caused populations of some finfish and shellfish to fall to dangerously low numbers. So catches of those species had to be limited at various times to give their populations time to recover. To aid in their recovery, state and federal wildlife agencies established hatcheries more than a century ago. This allowed young freshwater and saltwater fish, including shad, cod and flounders, to be raised from eggs and then released into rivers, lakes and ocean waters.

Yellowtail flounder – 15 to 18 in. – salt water

Smallmouth bass – 8 to 15 in. – fresh water

Ocean currents

Cape Cod is a general geographic meeting point for warm currents flowing north from the equator along the Atlantic Coast and colder currents flowing south from Canadian waters.

Certain fish, such as the Atlantic salmon and the Atlantic cod, prefer cold water and generally stay north of the Cape. However, others, such as the mako shark and the black sea bass, prefer warmer waters and can usually be found south of the Cape.

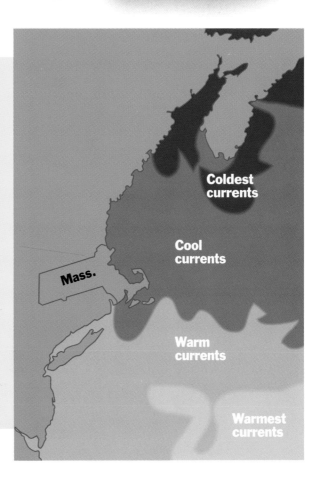

Coldest currents

Cool currents

Mass.

Warm currents

Warmest currents

Whales

Once, the ocean off Cape Cod was the destination for the ships of whale hunters. Now, those same waters are an attraction for the ships of whale watchers.

Finbacks and humpbacks, pilot whales and right whales – some 21 different species of whales have been seen in the area just a few miles north of Provincetown, one of the best spots in the Atlantic for sighting the largest of marine creatures.

What makes this possible is the fortunate creation of a dying glacier 18,500 years ago – Stellwagen Bank. This underwater plateau creates just the right conditions to feed an amazing range of whales and other ocean life.

The bank, about 20 miles long and 6 miles across at its widest point, is located between Cape Ann and Cape Cod. Its average depth is about 100 feet, but to the west and east of the bank, the ocean depth can drop off quickly, reaching 300 to 600 feet in places.

When the last glacier to cover New England was advancing, it reached all the way to Cape Cod. But as it melted, it dropped all the debris it had been carrying, including boulders, gravel and sand. These piles formed Stellwagen Bank and much of the Massachusetts coast.

Because the bank is a plateau with deeper waters all around it, ocean currents send nutrient-rich water from the deeper regions up the sides of the bank and onto the flat area on top. Here, closer to the

Humpback whale

Dolphin or porpoise?

● Dolphins, with their long snouts, are often more playful than porpoises and will usually venture closer to people and boats. Porpoises have shorter noses and tend to be shyer creatures than dolphins.

water's surface and the sunlight, the conditions are right for the growth of plankton, the microscopic plants and animals that larger marine creatures love to eat.

All this turns Stellwagen Bank into the ocean version of an all-you-can-eat buffet. Small fish eat the plankton and are in turn eaten by many whales. However, some whales, such as right whales, mainly eat the plankton.

The most common whales to be seen in Massachusetts Bay (other than dolphins and porpoises, which are types of small whales) are humpback and finback whales. Only rarely seen on the bank, perhaps once every four or five years, is a blue whale. The largest animal that has ever lived on earth, the blue whale can be more than 100 feet long and can weigh a half-million pounds.

Atlantic white-sided dolphins

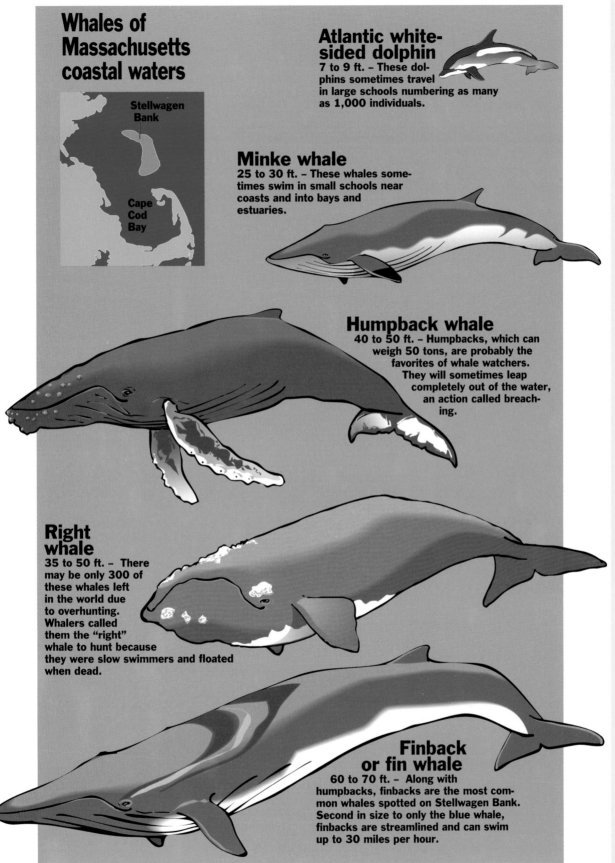

Whales of Massachusetts coastal waters

Stellwagen Bank

Cape Cod Bay

Atlantic white-sided dolphin
7 to 9 ft. – These dolphins sometimes travel in large schools numbering as many as 1,000 individuals.

Minke whale
25 to 30 ft. – These whales sometimes swim in small schools near coasts and into bays and estuaries.

Humpback whale
40 to 50 ft. – Humpbacks, which can weigh 50 tons, are probably the favorites of whale watchers. They will sometimes leap completely out of the water, an action called breaching.

Right whale
35 to 50 ft. – There may be only 300 of these whales left in the world due to overhunting. Whalers called them the "right" whale to hunt because they were slow swimmers and floated when dead.

Finback or fin whale
60 to 70 ft. – Along with humpbacks, finbacks are the most common whales spotted on Stellwagen Bank. Second in size to only the blue whale, finbacks are streamlined and can swim up to 30 miles per hour.

Wildlife in winter

In weather not fit for man or beast, the beasts and other forms of wildlife manage to do a pretty good job of surviving in winter.

Through the ages, they've gained a variety of tricks for getting through even the most severe winter weather.

Some hibernate, sleeping through the worst of it. Others know how and where to avoid biting winds and freezing temperatures and where to find food in a pinch.

Birds can seem the most vulnerable of animals in winter, but they often ride out storms perched high up inside the layered branches of dense evergreen trees, sheltered from the snow and wind, sleeping or eating insects they find in the bark and under limbs. Their feathers offer natural protection from the cold. They can also fluff up their feathers with air for even greater insulation.

Woodchucks and chipmunks hibernate through the winter in dens and burrows. For these and other mammals, their fur is their winter coat. Beavers spend the winter awake in their lodges. White-tailed deer gather together in "deer yards" deep in forests, and rabbits take refuge in tunnels under snow-covered shrubs or in abandoned woodchuck holes.

For coyotes, red foxes, bobcats and a variety of birds of prey, from eagles to great horned owls, winter in this region is business as usual as they prowl and patrol

Mallards

the countryside for a meal. Snow can actually benefit them as it can make prey that are on top of it stand out.

For both plants and animals, the greatest danger of severe cold is that it can freeze water. When water does freeze, it expands and can form sharp-edged ice crystals. The cells of all living things are filled with water, and if that water turns to ice, it can puncture the cell walls, causing damage or even death.

Some plants and animals create chemicals in and around their cells that act like

Winter survival strategies

Sugar maple
Leaf-bearing trees, such as maples, shed their frost-sensitive leaves in the fall and move a lot of their water and nutrients – their sap – into their roots, away from freezing temperatures.

White pine
The needles of evergreens, such as pines, are not very sensitive to cold because of natural antifreeze molecules within their cells. Also, the cells contain low amounts of water.

Day lily
Some plants, like corn, die completely at the first frost, leaving their seeds behind to produce new plants in the spring. In others, like day lilies, the parts above ground die when winter arrives, but underground roots and stems live to grow again in the spring.

Ice storm

antifreeze in a car, lowering the temperature at which water freezes.

Perhaps the most fantastic trick is the one some frogs use. Many frogs spend the winter on land, buried beneath leaves on the forest floor. But it may become so cold that even these places have freezing temperatures. To cope with such conditions, treefrogs, wood frogs and even spring peepers have found a way to turn to ice in winter, their bodies nearly frozen solid inside and out, and still survive. With just a few warm spring days, they will thaw out and begin to do the things frogs nor-

Gray squirrel

mally do in the spring.

How do animals manage to freeze and yet survive? They create chemical "seeds" within their body cavities but outside their cells. When the temperature drops below freezing, ice crystals will form around the seeds so that the water inside the cells does not freeze. Up to two-thirds of a frog's body water can freeze, yet it can remain alive because its cells are unharmed. In this way, frogs can withstand temperatures nearly 15 degrees below freezing for weeks or even months at a time.

Winter survival strategies

Honey bee
Honey bees form large clusters inside their hives and create heat by feeding on stores of honey. To prevent the bees on the outside of the cluster from freezing to death, those on the inside change places with them from time to time.

Flounder
Flounders and some other fish can produce their own antifreeze to keep their body fluids from freezing. Salt water freezes at a lower temperature than fresh water, so in Massachusetts coastal areas, fish that overwinter may be swimming in water with subfreezing temperatures.

Snapping turtle
These cold-blooded creatures will often sit in the mud at the bottoms of ponds, since the mud usually does not freeze in winter. There, they lower their heart beat and other body processes until they have almost no signs of life. They will live this way until spring.

Trees

Henry David Thoreau, the philosopher, was supposedly able to look out his back door in Concord in the mid-1800s and see all the way to Mount Monadnock in New Hampshire because there were so few trees to block his view.

In fact, in the early 1800s Massachusetts may have looked much like a farm state in the Midwest, such as Kansas or Indiana. Farm fields, barren of trees, stretched from horizon to horizon in many places in Massachusetts. Only about a fifth of the state was forested.

Why had so much land been cleared of trees? New England's Native Americans found they could more easily hunt animals in open areas than in thick forests, so they burned away many of the trees. And when Europeans settled in Massachusetts, they cleared more of the trees to create farm fields.

After the Civil War, though, many farmers in New England decided to leave their farms when they found they could not make a profit because of competition from farmers in the Midwest. Some moved west, seeking better land. Others moved to cities, seeking jobs. Gradually, open land in the state began to grow back into forests. Today, forests cover more than three of every five acres.

Massachusetts has a tremendous diversity of tree species in its forests – fir, spruce, hemlock, beech, red maple, white pine, red oak, green ash.

Farther north in New England, you will find mainly "coniferous" trees – evergreen trees bearing cones, such as pines and hemlocks. Farther south in New England and in the mid-Atlantic states, you will find mainly "deciduous" trees, leaf-bearing trees such as oaks and maples.

Massachusetts lies between these two zones and has many varieties of both coniferous and deciduous trees.

Trees, like animals, are involved in a continuing battle for survival. One species of tree may have to compete with another species to stay alive in the forest. For instance, one type of tree might grow higher in the forest than another, blocking the other's light and eventually killing off the shorter species.

When a hurricane or a fire creates an area of open land in this region, there is a predictable order in which seedlings will

Fall foliage

The forests of Massachusetts

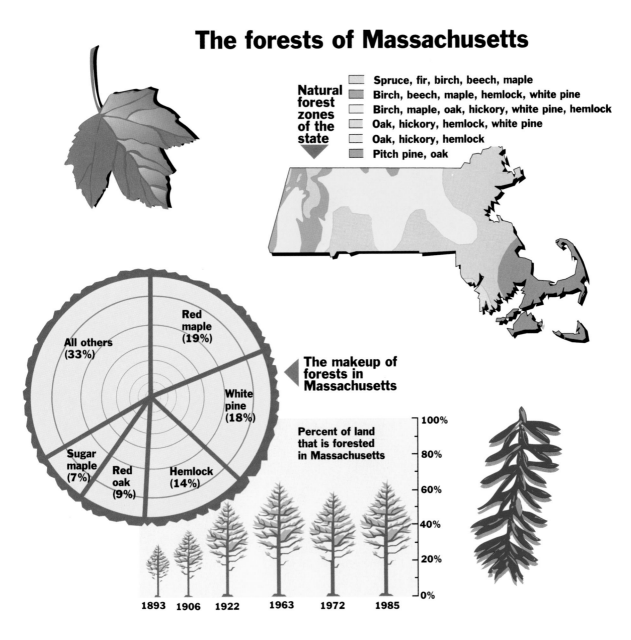

Natural forest zones of the state
- Spruce, fir, birch, beech, maple
- Birch, beech, maple, hemlock, white pine
- Birch, maple, oak, hickory, white pine, hemlock
- Oak, hickory, hemlock, white pine
- Oak, hickory, hemlock
- Pitch pine, oak

The makeup of forests in Massachusetts

- Red maple (19%)
- White pine (18%)
- Hemlock (14%)
- Red oak (9%)
- Sugar maple (7%)
- All others (33%)

Percent of land that is forested in Massachusetts

100% 80% 60% 40% 20% 0%

1893 1906 1922 1963 1972 1985

take root in the clearing. However, it may take more than two centuries for a forest that develops there to grow to its mature state.

Eastern white pine is usually the first species of tree to take root in an open field. Grazing animals, such as deer, like to eat the seedlings of hardwood trees, such as maples and oaks, but not the seedlings of pines, which are softwoods. (A softwood tree is just what its name suggests. The wood is softer than that of a hardwood tree.)

Once the pine forest begins maturing, the hardwoods will slowly take root beneath the umbrella formed by the pines.

Because the hardwoods can reproduce in shade, they flourish on the forest floor. But because pine cannot easily grow in shade, pine seedlings on the forest floor do not prosper. Eventually, the tall pines may die and the smaller hardwoods will grow to replace them.

In a mature forest in Southern New England, when a final balance is reached between all the species that have taken root and they are no longer competing with each other for a place in the forest, you might find white oak, red oak, hickory, beech and maple. In Northern New England a mature forest might contain spruce, maple, hemlock, birch and beech.

Most Massachusetts forests have not reached that final mature stage, however. Because so much land was cleared for farming in the 1800s, and because the great hurricane of 1938 leveled much of the state's timberland, most of the forests are still in a middle stage in their development.

Only a few hundred acres of true "old-growth" forests exist in the state, mainly on remote slopes of the Berkshire Hills, although a few stands were recently found on Wachusett Mountain in Princeton. These forests are more than two centuries old. Some trees in them were alive before George Washington was born.

Trees depend on soil to anchor their roots and provide nutrients to help

Northern red oak acorns

them grow. As the type and depth of soil changes from region to region, so will the trees you see. In rocky, mountainous regions, such as on the slopes of Mount Watatic in Ashburnham where the depth of soil to the underlying bedrock is often shallow, you tend to find paper birches or eastern hemlocks. Where the soil is moist, as in the flood plain of the Concord River, you are likely to find trees such as red maples or eastern sycamores.

On Cape Cod and the islands, where the soil is sandy and dry, you will likely find a different group of trees, which grow lower to the ground, such as pitch pines and post oaks. Some oak trees on the Cape grow so low that they may look like shrubs.

Old-growth forests in Massachusetts

Old-growth trees in the state are located in Western Massachusetts and on Wachusett Mountain in Princeton.

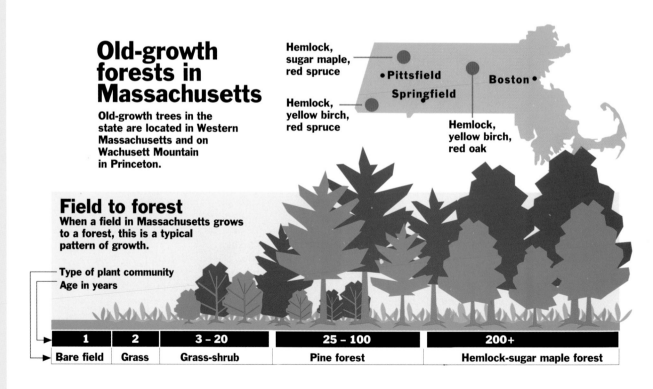

Hemlock, sugar maple, red spruce

Hemlock, yellow birch, red spruce

•Pittsfield

Springfield

Boston •

Hemlock, yellow birch, red oak

Field to forest
When a field in Massachusetts grows to a forest, this is a typical pattern of growth.

Type of plant community
Age in years

1	2	3 – 20	25 – 100	200+
Bare field	Grass	Grass-shrub	Pine forest	Hemlock-sugar maple forest

Fall foliage – just an accident?

Perhaps nature's most brilliant artistic touch, the scarlets and golds of autumn leaves may also be one of nature's most beautiful accidents.

The startling colors of fall are certainly admired by human beings. But the colors seem to defy one of nature's primary laws, which is that they are of no use to the trees themselves.

Most plants and animals have the features they have because those features help them survive in the world. In plants, color developed in flowers as a way to attract pollinators such as bees and butterflies. Seeds surrounded by colorful, tasty fruits are also a feature plants use to attract animals, which eat the fruits and spread the seeds to other places.

But what use is a colorful leaf to a tree in autumn since the leaf is just about to die and fall to the ground?

Scientists believe that autumn colors may have begun as an accident, the unexpected result of the chemical changes a tree goes through as it prepares to lose its leaves each fall.

But even if it was an accident, since this coloring causes no harm to the trees, there is no reason for trees to lose this process. If the coloring did cause harm, those species of trees whose leaves changed color might have become extinct by now, and only the trees whose leaves didn't change color might be alive today.

Approximate times for peak foliage colors

Oct. 1–14

Oct. 3–16

Oct. 5–18

Oct. 15–21

Oct. 17–24

70 – 100 ft.

Sugar maple – Perhaps the best known tree in New England, its sap is used to make maple syrup, and its leaves turn vivid colors in autumn.

60 – 90 ft.

Red maple – In the spring, red and orange flowers appear at the ends of the twigs before red leaves appear and eventually turn green.

50 – 100 ft.

Northern red oak – This fast-growing tree is an important source both of acorns that feed wildlife and of strong wood for furniture.

70 – 100 ft.

Yellow birch – Like the paper birch, the yellow birch has bark that may peel into strips. This birch prefers rich woods in upland areas.

40 – 60 ft.

Green ash – A fast-growing tree, the green ash produces tough, light-brown wood that is often used to make ax handles and baskets.

60 – 90 ft.

Black cherry – The bark of black cherry trees is used to produce cough syrup, and the fruit of the trees is used to make jelly and wine.

40 – 60 ft.

Black locust – A rapidly growing tree, the black locust may look like the honeylocust, but the black locust is usually shorter and less thorny.

60 – 100 ft.

American sycamore – Sycamores prefer the wet soil of stream banks, flood plains and the edges of marshes and other wetlands.

70 – 120 ft.

Shagbark hickory – Identified by its distinctive shaggy bark, this tree has strong wood that is used to make baseball bats.

60 – 90 ft.

American beech – A popular shade tree, the beech produces beechnuts, which are eaten by a range of wildlife, including squirrels, bears and chipmunks.

50 – 80 ft.

Paper birch – Used by Native Americans to create birchbark canoes, paper birches have white bark that may come off the trees in coiled strips.

30 – 50 ft.

Weeping willow – These willows, natives of China, often grow in moist soils by ponds or lakes. Their leaves are among the first to appear in spring.

100 – 150 ft.

Eastern white pine – The largest conifer in the East, white pine, with its long, straight trunk, was used to produce masts for colonial sailing ships.

40 – 60 ft.

Pitch pine – These pines prefer the dry, sandy soil found in coastal areas. They are rich in resins used by European colonists to make turpentine and tar.

40 – 60 ft.

Eastern red cedar – The fragrant reddish wood of the red cedar is often used to build furniture such as cedar chests and cabinets.

60 – 80 ft.

Eastern hemlock – This evergreen often grows in cool valleys and on hillsides. Its branches were used by early European settlers to make brooms.

70 – 90 ft.

Norway spruce – A large conifer, the Norway spruce was native to Europe. Like most conifers, it grows best in cool temperatures.

40 – 60 ft.

Balsam fir – The only native fir of the Northeast, the balsam fir is often chosen as a Christmas tree. Deer will eat its twigs and needles in winter.

Street trees

You have to be tough to grow up on the streets of a city, and that includes trees. Air pollution, trash and poor soil are just a few of the things trees have to deal with in the urban jungle. Here are some species of trees that are often chosen to line city streets because of their ability to handle urban stresses.

60 – 80 ft.

Littleleaf linden – A popular shade tree, this species grows in a pleasing shape and produces yellowish clusters of flowers attractive to bees.

50 – 70 ft.

Norway maple – A native of Europe, the Norway maple tolerates partial shade, poor soil, heat, drought, dust, smoke and insect pests.

60 – 90 ft.

Honeylocust – The honeylocust, which tolerates heat and drought, is distinctive because of the thorns or spines that grow in clumps on its trunk.

60 – 90 ft.

London planetree – A cross between the American sycamore and an Oriental planetree, this variety grows quickly into a large shade tree.

30 – 50 ft.

Bradford pear – A native of China, the Bradford pear produces a mass of white flowers in the spring. It is tolerant of pollution and insects.

20 – 30 ft.

Flowering crabapple – Grown in hundreds of varieties, the flowering crabapple produces beautiful white, pink or red flowers in spring.

Wildflowers

Impressionist painters would not have gotten far without wildflowers.

Wildflowers were art before there was art – dashes of color on canvases of windblown meadows, craggy mountainsides and darkened forest floors.

Even their names are poetic – Jack-in-the-pulpit, Queen Anne's lace, butter-and-eggs, pink lady's slipper.

But as unplanned as a scattering of wildflowers may seem, where and when they bloom and the colors and shapes they take follow a precise logic. Much of that logic has to do with helping each species of wildflower find its own place in the world.

If all wildflowers bloomed at the same time, grew in the same soil and sunlight conditions, and attracted the same pollinators, the fierce competition would mean that only a few species would survive. So wildflowers evolved to be specialists. Some grow only in wet areas, some grow only in dry areas. Some thrive in valleys and others on mountainsides. Some can grow where there is a lot of sunlight, as in a meadow, while others can grow where there is little of it, as on a forest floor.

To further reduce competition, wildflowers also evolved to bloom at different times of year. Common violets bloom in April and May, but New England asters don't bloom until September and October.

The beauty of wildflowers is not something created to please the human eye. It actually evolved to appeal to

Fragrant water lily

Wild lupine

pollinators – butterflies, bees, ants, moths and even small birds, such as hummingbirds. Like neon signs outside a row of stores competing for passing customers, the splashy and bold colors of some wildflowers are designed to attract pollinators to them, as are the fragrances the flowers give off and the sweet nectar produced inside the flowers.

A wildflower needs to get the pollen that the male part of the flower creates to the female part of another wildflower of the same species so that seeds can be created and new plants can grow. And pollinators are the pollen carriers.

If a butterfly visits a flower to feed on the nectar deep inside the flower, tiny grains of pollen may stick to it and be carried to the next flower it visits.

The varied shapes and colors of wildflowers also evolved to let a pollinator know exactly what kind of flower it is. Most pollinators can recognize certain shapes and patterns of color, so if they like the nectar they found at a flower, they will know to visit that same type of flower again. In this way, pollen from an evening primrose has a way of getting to another evening primrose, rather than ending up on a black-eyed Susan.

The bull's-eye shape of many flowers evolved to guide the pollinator to the

Wildflower or weed?

● There is no official definition for which is which. Weeds are usually thought of as the wildflowers that people, for some reason, don't like. Some people think dandelions are weeds because they can take over a lawn. But others like their colorful flowers and think of them as wildflowers.

nectar. "Here it is – right at the center," this shape seems to say. Other wildflowers have a shape like the end of a trumpet for the same reason. "The nectar is right inside here – you can't miss it," this shape seems to say.

In Massachusetts, there are nearly 1,500 different types of wildflowers that can be found through the seasons. However, some of the most common wildflowers in the state today are not native to Massachusetts. Oxeye daisies, red clover and bouncing Bet were brought here from Europe.

Bloom times for Massachusetts wildflowers

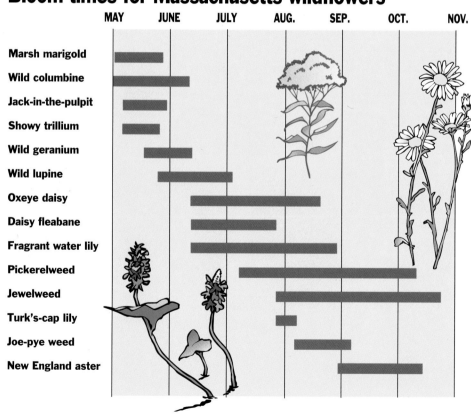

	MAY	JUNE	JULY	AUG.	SEP.	OCT.	NOV.
Marsh marigold							
Wild columbine							
Jack-in-the-pulpit							
Showy trillium							
Wild geranium							
Wild lupine							
Oxeye daisy							
Daisy fleabane							
Fragrant water lily							
Pickerelweed							
Jewelweed							
Turk's-cap lily							
Joe-pye weed							
New England aster							

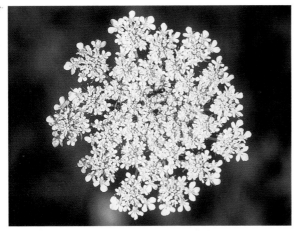

Queen Anne's lace - June to Sept. - Flower clusters 3 to 7 in. wide - Also called wild carrots, these lacy flowers grow on roadsides and in fields.

Oxeye daisy - June to Aug. - Flowers 1 to 2 in. wide - The most familiar wildflower of fields and meadows, this daisy is a European native.

Fragrant water lily - June to Sept. - Flowers 3 to 5 in. wide - The striking flowers of this water lily usually bloom from morning to noon.

Wood anemone - May - Flowers about 1 in. wide - Wood anemones often bloom near the edges of woods, growing close to the ground.

Large-flowered trillium - May - Flowers 2 to 4 in. wide - Also called showy trillium, this is a wildflower of the deep woods.

Bouncing Bet - July and Aug. - Flowers about 1 in. wide - This wildflower tends to grow on roadsides and in fields, spreading by underground stems.

Skunk cabbage – April and May – Flowers 3 to 6 in. long – This wetland wildflower blooms in early spring. It can give off a foul odor when crushed.

Cattail – May to July – Flowers about 6 in. long – Cattails grow in thick stands in shallow water, providing nesting habitat for various birds.

Spotted Joe-pye weed – Aug. and Sept. – Flower clusters 3 to 6 in. wide – Used as a medicine in colonial times, this wildflower grows in damp soil.

Jack-in-the-pulpit – May and June – Flowers 3 to 4 in. long – This spring wildflower grows in the moist soil of woods, swamps and marshes.

Beach heath – May to July – Flowers .3 in. wide – As its name implies, beach heath can usually be found on sand dunes and in thin coastal soils.

Tall goldenrod – Aug. to Oct. – Flowers about .2 in. long – Up to 7 feet tall, these plants are common along roads and in fields in late summer.

Common dandelion – April to Sept. – Flowers about 1.5 in. wide – Considered a weed by many, it is often seen on lawns, in fields and along roads.

Black-eyed Susan – June to Sept. – Flowers 2 to 3 in. wide – A member of the sunflower family, this flower grows in just about any open place.

Common buttercup – May and June – Flowers about 1 in. wide – Buttercups are harsh tasting to animals, which gives them more chance to spread.

Evening primrose – June to Aug. – Flowers 1 to 2 in. wide – The evening primrose opens its flowers in the evening and closes them by noon.

Butter-and-eggs – June to Sept. – Flowers about 1 in. long – A native of Europe, butter-and-eggs can sprout in almost any open place.

Marsh marigold – May – Flowers 1 to 1.5 in. wide – These yellow flowers bloom in wet habitats, such as marshes and swamps, in the spring.

Yellow lady's slipper – May and June – Flowers about 2 in. long – These popular orchids are vanishing in the wild and should not be picked.

Turk's-cap lily – July and Aug. – Flowers 2 to 3 in. wide – This beautiful lily grows on tall stalks, up to 7 feet high, in wet fields and swamps.

Day lily – June and July – Flowers 3 to 4 in. wide – This was a garden flower that escaped and flourished in the wild, often growing on roadsides.

Jewelweed – July to Oct. – Flowers about 1 in. long – Also called spotted touch-me-not, this delicate wildflower prefers moist soil.

Wild columbine – May and June – Flowers about 2 in. long – A woodland wildflower, wild columbine tends to grow on rocky or open slopes.

Rugosa rose – June to Aug. – Flowers 2 to 3 in. wide – This rose, a native of the Orient, blooms on beaches and coastal dunes.

Red clover – June to Aug. – Flowers .5 to 1 in. wide – Red clover grows close to the ground in fields, on lawns and on roadsides.

Bull thistle – July and Aug. – Flowers about 2 in. wide – Bull thistle has sharp spines on its stem. It's usually found in meadows and along roadsides.

Common milkweed – June to Aug. – Flowers about .5 in. wide – Monarch butterflies seek out milkweed to lay their eggs on the leaves.

Common blue violet – April to June – Flowers .5 to 1 in. wide – These violets grow close to the ground in fields, meadows and along roadsides.

Pickerelweed – July to Oct. – Flowers about .3 in. long – Pickerelweed, with its blue-violet stalks, grows in the shallows of ponds, lakes and streams.

Purple loosestrife – July to Sept. – Flowers about .5 in. wide – A native of Europe and Asia, loosestrife often crowds out native wildflowers in wetlands.

Chicory – June to Aug. – Flowers 1 to 2 in. wide – The roots of this roadside and field flower are roasted in some places as a coffee substitute.

Wild geranium – May and June – Flowers 1 to 2 in. wide – These fragile-looking lavender flowers grow in fields and forest openings.

New England aster – Sept. and Oct. – Flowers 1 to 2 in. wide – Most asters, which come in many varieties, bloom late in the season.

Daisy fleabane – June and July – Flowers about 1 in. wide – Daisy, or common, fleabane may look like an aster, but it blooms earlier in the season.

Wild lupine – May to July – Flowers about .7 in. long – The colorful stalks of wild lupine are usually seen in fields, woodland clearings and sandy soils.

Blue flag – May to July – Flowers 3 to 4 in. wide – These beautiful irises grow along the shores of ponds, lakes, swamps and marshes.

Ecosystems

Same planet, different worlds.

That's a good definition of ecosystems, the largely self-contained collections of plants, animals and ecological conditions that cover the landscape like different countries on a map.

A pond with bullfrogs, cattails and dragonflies can be near a forest where you might see hemlocks, wolf spiders and white-tailed deer. And just a stone's throw away can be a meadow where you might find monarch butterflies, oxeye daisies and meadow voles.

An ecosystem provides a specific kind of wildlife habitat that is home to many of the same plants and animals wherever that kind of ecosystem can be found. An ecosystem is created by different combinations of water, land features, sunlight, temperature and vegetation. And different combinations of those elements will create different kinds of ecosystems containing different plant and animal species.

An ecosystem can be a stream or a pond, or it can be a combination of a stream and a pond. An ecosystem can be a meadow in a valley or a meadow on a mountainside.

An ecosystem can be as small as a single pool of water left from melted snow on a forest floor in spring, or it can be as large as the whole forest, including the pool of water.

Ecosystems are also found in cities. A vacant lot between two buildings may eventually become home to a variety of wildflowers, insects, birds and small mammals. A line of trees along a sidewalk is also an ecosystem, attracting specific kinds of insects and birds.

Ecosystems do not have barriers between them, though. They overlap and share resources. Insects, birds and other animals move between ecosystems. And a stream that is part of a forest ecosystem may also flow into and be part of a nearby meadow ecosystem.

In nature, plants and animals depend on each other for food. Many birds eat insects. Many insects eat the leaves of trees and other plants. Trees and other plants draw nutrition through their roots from dead plants and animals that decay on the ground. This is called a food web.

After a long period of time, a balance or a harmony in the food web in an ecosystem is often reached so that populations of the different species stay within certain limits. If the population of one species grows too large, it may run out of food, or another species that feeds on it may

A beaver pond may come and go as beavers come and go. So the species of plants and animals that live in this kind of ecosystem tend to change as the conditions of the pond change.

A beaver's diet is tree bark, and it uses trees to build dams and its lodge. Once the supply of their favorite trees is used up, beavers will abandon the pond, their dam will fall apart and the water will drain away. The pond may then revert to an ecosystem of a meadow with a stream running through it. Eventually, the trees may grow back and beavers may return, turning the meadow into a pond once again.

Animals you may see in and around a beaver pond include beavers, red-spotted newts, painted turtles, water snakes, snapping turtles, dragonflies, damselflies, green frogs, bullfrogs, herons, mallards and raccoons.

Food web

In any ecosystem, an interrelationship develops between plants and animals in regard to food, and it is called a food web. Plants get much of their energy to grow from the sun, some insects eat live and dead plant matter, some small animals eat insects, and some large animals eat small animals.

In a forest ecosystem where oak trees abound, acorns and other nuts are an important part of the food web. Here is just a part of the food web in such a forest.

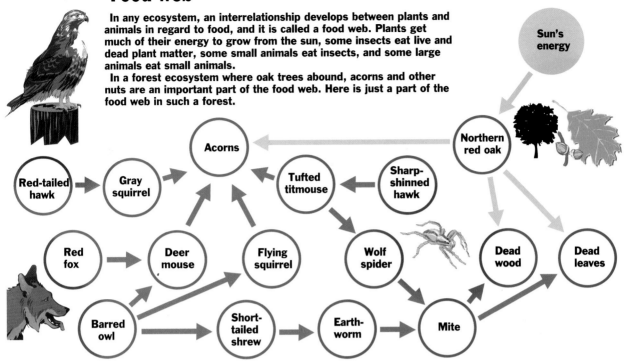

reduce its population.

For instance, if the muskrat population of a marsh grows large, minks, which feed on muskrats, may increase in numbers around the marsh because there is more food for the minks and their young. But once the muskrat population is reduced by the minks, fewer minks will be able to survive or they will have to move to another marsh because there is no longer enough food for all of them. Soon, their population will decline around the marsh, and the muskrat population will have a chance to grow once again.

A meadow tends to be a changing ecosystem, quickly growing to shrubs and then into a young forest. A meadow may be created when a fire destroys a forest or when a beaver abandons its pond and the water drains away. A meadows can also be created when a farmer abandons a farm and the fields have a chance to return to a wild state.

Wildlife populations in many ecosystems change with the seasons. In a meadow, wildflowers bloom at different times of year, and many birds visit meadows only during the nesting season.

Animals you might see in or around a meadow include eastern cottontails, green snakes, meadow voles, field sparrows, bobolinks, red-tailed hawks, American kestrels, striped skunks, red foxes, woodchucks and white-tailed deer.

Weather

Mark Twain claimed to have counted 136 different kinds of weather in New England during just 24 hours.

He may have been joking, but the region can indeed offer some dramatic weather extremes, from hail in July and nor'easters in December to tornadoes, floods, hurricanes and droughts.

As complicated as New England's weather may seem, though, much of it comes down to the classic confrontation of two weather systems – cold dry air blowing down from Canada in the north and warm moist air blowing up off the Atlantic Ocean from the southeast. It is this climatological clash, often occurring right over New England, that produces much of the irregular weather seen on a regular basis in the region.

The coldest weather often occurs when frigid Canadian air flows down into the region in winter and no warm southern air gets in its way. The most humid weather usually happens in summer when tropical air blows directly up from the southeast.

Because of normal wind patterns, though, New England is frequently a battleground for these warm and cold air masses. To understand how their coming together affects New England, a few basic laws of physics need to be understood.

First, hot air tends to rise and cold air tends to sink. This is because hot air is lighter than an equal volume of cold air.

When air heats up, the molecules in it move around more, bumping into each other and increasing the space between them. That means that a cubic foot of hot air has fewer molecules in it and therefore less weight to it than the same volume of cold air. As a result, steam rises off a cooking pot on a stove, and the coldest air in an air-conditioned room is probably found near the floor.

What this means, weatherwise, is that if a mass of hot air and a mass of cold air come together, the hot air will rise to the top and the cold air will sink to the bottom.

Despite this, the temperature is cooler the higher you go up in the atmosphere. All air, hot or cold, cools by about 5.4°F for every 1,000 feet it rises in the atmosphere. (Falling air warms up at the same rate.) That's why the air temperature at the top of a mountain is cooler than at the bottom.

Because hot air tends to rise, a mass of hot air on the ground will press down on the ground with less force than a mass of cold air. When you hear the term "high-pressure system," it usually means a weather system of colder air. A "low-pressure system" is usually one made up of warmer air.

One of the results of all these laws is a nor'easter, a powerful storm that can sweep into New England. In winter, a

Sunset

nor'easter can blanket the region with snow.

A nor'easter can form when a warmer air mass loaded with moisture comes up off the ocean into New England, where it bumps into a colder Canadian air mass coming down from the north. The warmer air mass shoots up into the atmosphere, where its temperature cools to below freezing and the moisture in it turns to snow, which falls over New England.

Another physical law to know is that a mass of cold air will generally create winds around it that are clockwise in

motion when viewed from above. A mass of warm air will create counterclockwise winds. This has to do with the air pressures in and around the air masses and with the rotation of the earth.

The result of this can be a weather pattern that can create warm, humid days in New England in summer. A high-pressure system moves out over the Atlantic Ocean and stalls there because of the lack of winds to push it any farther. It creates clockwise winds that, like a huge fan, push warm tropical air back up into New England.

Nor'easter

In winter, this classic snowstorm can occur as often as once a week in New England from December through March. The storm can form when arctic air meets warmer moist air coming up from the south.

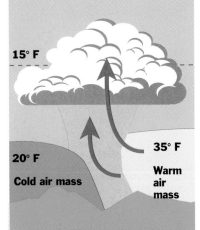

1. At the front, where the cold and warm air masses meet, the heavier cold air pushes under the warmer air, which rises in streams into the atmosphere.

2. As the warmer air goes higher in the atmosphere, it cools and cannot hold as much water. The excess water becomes tiny droplets, which turn to snow in the freezing temperatures at that altitude.

3. The buildup of snow in the upper atmosphere becomes so great that the weight of it eventually causes the snowflakes to fall to the ground.

Summer storm

This can be a fast-moving, violent storm. A cold air mass from Canada comes into New England from the northwest. Meanwhile, a warm, moist, tropical air mass moves into the area from off the Atlantic Ocean to the south.

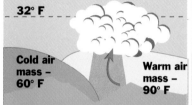

32° F

Cold air mass – 60° F

Warm air mass – 90° F

Noon

At the front, where the air masses meet, the heavier colder air slides under the lighter warmer air, sending streams of hot, moist air into the atmosphere, where clouds of water droplets form.

12:20 p.m.

High in the atmosphere, the temperature is below freezing, and the water droplets turn to ice and snow, darkening the clouds.

Cold air mass – 60° F Warm air mass – 90° F

12:40 p.m.

The ice and snow become so heavy that they begin to fall, turning to rain in the warmer air below. The updrafts of hot air and downdrafts of rain creates violent winds.

Cold air mass – 60° F Warm air mass – 90° F

1 p.m.

The storm ends when the downdrafts of rain eventually smother the updrafts. Also, the two air masses move out of the area.

Cold air mass – 60° F Warm air mass – 90° F

Ice storm

In the fall, a Canadian cold air mass with freezing temperatures collides with a warmer air mass coming up off the ocean.

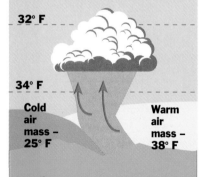
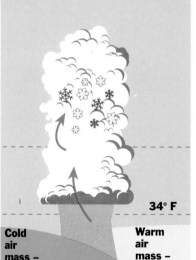
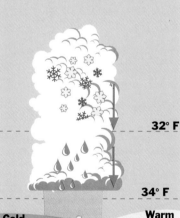

32° F

34° F

Cold air mass – 25° F   Warm air mass – 38° F

1. At the front, the heavier, colder air pushes under the warmer air, which rises into the atmosphere.

Cold air mass – 25° F   Warm air mass – 38° F

2. The rising warmer air creates clouds of water droplets that turn to ice and snow.

32° F

34° F

Cold air mass – 25° F   Warm air mass – 38° F

3. The ice and snow begin to fall. They turn to rain in the warmer temperatures below but then turn to ice when they enter the cold air mass.

Clouds

Summer swelter

Sometimes in summer, it can seem that New England is located in the tropics. Hot, humid weather settles on this region and won't seem to go away.

It can happen when a high-pressure system (a mass of air that is colder and therefore heavier than the surrounding air) is located to the southeast of New England, over the Atlantic Ocean.

Called a Bermuda high (because it is often centered near the island of Bermuda), the air mass creates winds around it that flow clockwise. These winds push humid, tropical air toward New England.

Oftentimes during summer, there is a lack of strong winds in that region of the Atlantic, so the Bermuda high may not move for a week or more. That means New England can count on the uncomfortable summer swelter to last at least that long.

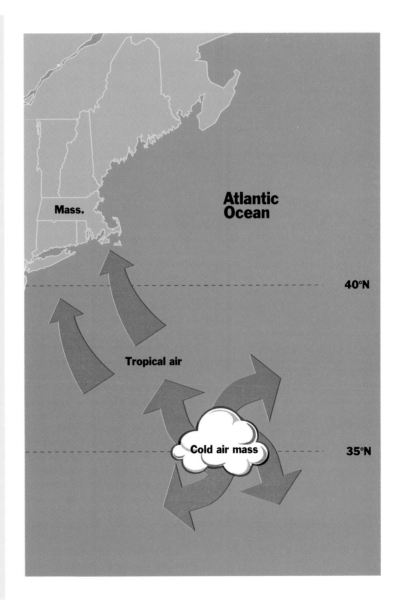

Lightning

Lightning can streak within clouds, from cloud to cloud, and from clouds to the ground. Like sparks that fly when a sweater is rubbed, lightning is created by a difference in electrical charges. It is often a flow of current between a strong negative charge in the clouds and a strong positive charge in the ground.

1. In the clouds, there is a buildup of electrons, which are negatively charged. Some electrons begin traveling toward the ground.

2. As the stream of electrons nears the ground, it begins to draw a stream of positive charge from the ground.

3. When the two streams come together, a powerful current begins flowing.

4. A positively charged flow shoots up into the clouds, traveling at about 60,000 miles per second. This is the light we see in a lightning strike.

Thunder

Thunder is the sound lightning creates as it superheats the air directly around it to as much as 45,000°F. The heat causes the air to expand rapidly, sending out a shock wave that becomes a crack of thunder when it reaches the human ear. The sound moves about a mile every five seconds. So if you see a flash of lightning and then hear the thunder five seconds later, the strike is about a mile away.

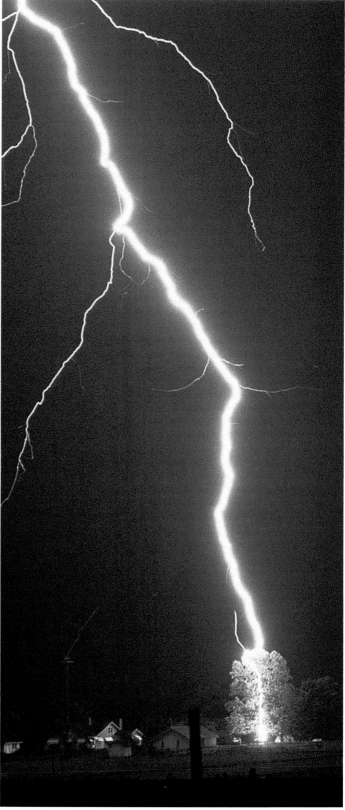

Lightning strike

Clouds

With any imagination, they're fleets of sailboats, parades of white elephants or herds of Arabian stallions passing overhead. Clouds are whatever you want them to be. But in fact, they're water – billions of tiny water droplets or ice crystals that have formed around microscopic particles in the atmosphere.

Clouds form when air rises in the atmosphere and cools. Air holds water, much like a sponge holds water. Water molecules are mixed in with molecules of oxygen, nitrogen

and other elements of the air we breathe.

When air cools, though, it cannot hold as many water molecules and they are squeezed out, like water squeezed from a sponge. These water molecules seek out particles of dust, such as salt from the ocean or bits of pollution, to attach to. And if enough water molecules attach to the same particle, they will become a visible droplet. And if enough visible droplets form, they will become a cloud.

Fog

Fog is really a cloud close to the ground. Like clouds, fog forms when warm moist air cools enough for the moisture in it to condense, forming tiny water droplets that float about in the air.

New England is actually one of the foggier regions of the United States. Cape Cod and northern Worcester County have an average of more than 40 days of heavy fog each year.

River or lake fog

In the spring, water is usually colder than the air. So fog will form on a water surface when the warmer air hits the surface, cools, and releases the moisture in it.

Mountain fog

When a mountain is beside a river or lake, air blowing over the water picks up moisture, then blows up the mountain slope, cooling as it rises, and releasing the moisture in it.

Snowflakes

Snowflakes are works of art, nearly weightless jewels of ice, but they are also deep mysteries. Scientists don't really have a clear understanding of why they take the shapes they do. For instance, why do snowflakes take certain shapes at certain temperatures and other shapes at other temperatures? And how can each of the six arms of a star-shaped snowflake be identical in its pattern, yet this pattern will vary from snowflake to snowflake?

Snowflakes, like diamonds and emeralds, are crystals. And all crystals are made up of repeating patterns of atoms or molecules.

Snowflakes are made up of water molecules that crystallize in freezing temperatures. To start the formation of a crystal, a water molecule must first attach to a solid particle in the air, such as a microscopic bit of ocean salt. Once it's attached, other water molecules will join it, and the crystal will begin to grow.

The crystal that develops can be shaped like a plate, needle, column or star, depending on the temperature of the air in which it forms. Whatever the form of the snowflake, the crystal will usually have six sides.

32° to 25°F	25° to 21°F	21° to 14°F	14° to 10°F	10° to 3°F	3° to -8°F	Below -8°F
Thin plates	Needles	Hollow columns	Sector plates	Dendrites	Sector plates	Hollow columns

Hurricanes

These ferocious storms originate in tropical waters, but they can sometimes find their way into New England.

Several hundred miles wide, and often packing winds of more than 100 miles per hour, hurricanes can wreak havoc in coastal areas of New England and often have enough power in them to still do significant damage as they move inland.

Hurricanes are not strictly summertime events. In fact, most of the serious hurricanes that have hit New England have done so after Labor Day. Nearly half (43 percent) have struck in September. The next most likely months are August (27 percent) and October (24 percent). Only a few (6 percent) have hit in July.

Hurricanes that strike New England have a typical path. It begins either in the Caribbean or on the other side of the Atlantic Ocean near the African coast. If winds, air pressure and water temperatures are right, a hurricane – a huge spiraling system of air currents that converts the heat of evaporating ocean water to powerful winds – may form.

If the storm begins off the west African coast, it may gradually move across the Atlantic, staying just north of the equator, steered by tropical trade winds. It then may curve up over the Caribbean, along the U.S. East Coast, and ultimately into New England.

A hurricane needs the energy of warm, moist, evaporating ocean water to keep its strength. Once a hurricane moves inland, its winds usually begin to die quickly. That's why most of the damage from hurricanes and the greatest number of deaths caused by them have been along or near the coast.

A hurricane's strength may also be drained as it moves north in the Atlantic, where ocean temperatures are usually cooler than in the tropics. For this reason, only about one in 20 hurricanes that strike the Caribbean goes on to strike New England.

Hurricane, tropical storm or just a really bad rainstorm?

● To qualify as a hurricane, a storm must have strong winds rotating about a moving center, and it must have sustained winds (as opposed to momentary wind gusts) of 74 miles per hour or more. If a storm has rotating winds that have speeds less than 74 mph and more than 39 mph, then it's a tropical storm. If a storm doesn't meet any of these requirements, then consider it just a severe rainstorm.

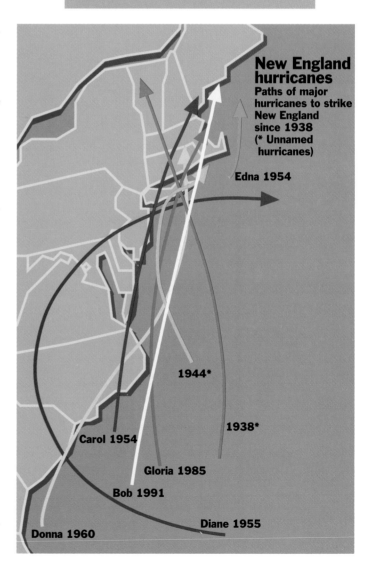

New England hurricanes
Paths of major hurricanes to strike New England since 1938 (* Unnamed hurricanes)

Edna 1954
1944*
1938*
Carol 1954
Gloria 1985
Bob 1991
Diane 1955
Donna 1960

The hurricane of 1938

Some called it "The Long Island Express." The hurricane that slammed into New England on Sept. 21, 1938, was the most destructive in the region's history. It killed nearly 600 people in the six states. It destroyed many coastal areas, reducing shoreline homes and businesses to rubble. And it had enough lingering power once it moved inland to level whole forests. As many as 250 million trees were toppled in the region by the furious winds.

It was a hurricane that moved so fast it hit many areas without warning.

The storm had been tracked for days. On Sept. 19, it had been threatening Florida, but its speed over water was only 15 miles per hour. A day later, though, as it headed up the coast, it gradually began to pick up speed. In fact, as it passed New Jersey and headed over Long Island toward New England, it was moving at more than 50 miles per hour.

Although the eye of the storm moved rapidly up the Connecticut River Valley, the hurricane's great force was felt throughout the state. On the crest of Great Blue Hill in Milton, winds gusted to 186 miles per hour.

The greatest damage was done along the coasts of Massachusetts and Rhode Island where the storm coincided with a high tide. Waves that pounded the beaches and crushed shoreline homes reached heights of 30 to 40 feet.

New England's deadliest tornado

On the evening of June 9, 1953, many people were just getting out of work and others were just sitting down to dinner when the deadliest tornado in New England's history struck in Massachusetts.

In a little more than an hour, the terrible tornado cut a 46-mile path through 11 communities that was a mile wide in places. The twister's winds reached 250 miles per hour.

The funnel cloud set down in Petersham, near Quabbin Reservoir, about 4:25 p.m. and by the time the destruction ended in Southborough around 5:40 p.m., 94 people lay dead, nearly 1,300 were injured and 10,000 were homeless.

In Worcester alone, 62 people were killed and 1,000 homes were demolished. Some residential streets were leveled, with not a chimney left standing. Many other homes were picked up off their foundations and tossed in the air.

The tornado proved to be the costliest in U.S. history up to that point, causing an estimated $53 million in damages.

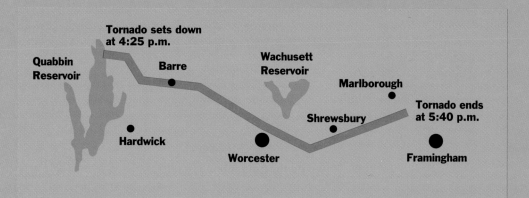

Average daily temperatures (°F)

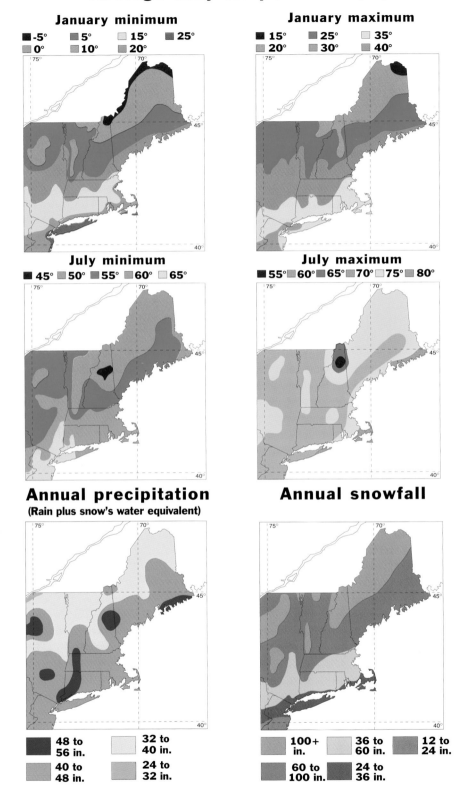

January minimum

■ -5° ■ 5° □ 15° ■ 25°
■ 0° ■ 10° ■ 20°

January maximum

■ 15° ■ 25° □ 35°
■ 20° ■ 30° ■ 40°

July minimum

■ 45° ■ 50° ■ 55° ■ 60° □ 65°

July maximum

■ 55° ■ 60° ■ 65° ■ 70° □ 75° ■ 80°

Annual precipitation

(Rain plus snow's water equivalent)

| ■ | 48 to 56 in. | □ | 32 to 40 in. |
| ■ | 40 to 48 in. | ■ | 24 to 32 in. |

Annual snowfall

| ■ | 100+ in. | □ | 36 to 60 in. | ■ | 12 to 24 in. |
| ■ | 60 to 100 in. | ■ | 24 to 36 in. | | |

These are general temperature and precipitation guides. Local measurements may differ sharply depending on such things as elevation, position in relation to mountains or large water bodies, and the urbanization of the area.

Sunrise and sunset in Eastern Massachusetts

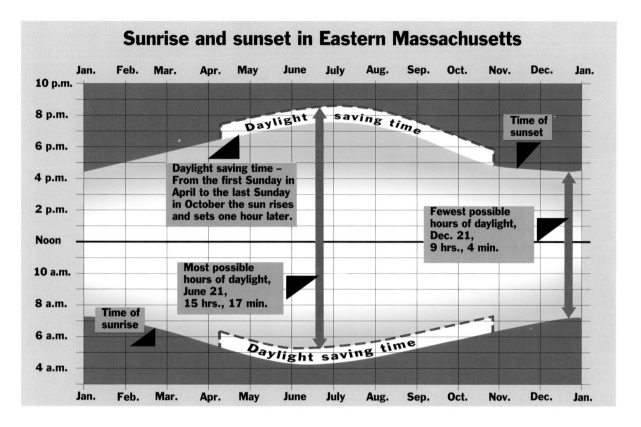

BOSTON	Jan.	Feb.	Mar.	Apr.	May	June	July	Aug.	Sep.	Oct.	Nov.	Dec.	Total or annual avg.
Snowfall (inches)	12.3	11.3	7.4	.9	0	0	0	0	0	0	1.4	7.5	40.8
Precipitation (inches)	3.99	3.70	4.13	3.73	3.52	2.92	2.68	3.68	3.41	3.36	4.21	4.48	43.8
Avg. daily max. temp.	36.4	37.7	45	56.6	67	76.6	81.8	79.8	72.3	62.5	51.6	40.3	59
Avg. daily min. temp.	22.8	23.7	31.8	40.8	50	59.3	65.1	63.9	56.9	47.1	38.7	27.1	43.9
Clear days (avg.)*	9	8	8	7	6	7	7	9	10	11	8	9	99
Cloudy days (avg.)**	15	13	15	15	15	13	12	11	12	12	15	15	162

WORCESTER	Jan.	Feb.	Mar.	Apr.	May	June	July	Aug.	Sep.	Oct.	Nov.	Dec.	Total or annual avg.
Snowfall (inches)	16.9	16.3	13.6	4.0	0	0	0	0	0	.6	3.8	13.0	68.6
Precipitation (inches)	3.82	3.29	4.16	3.90	3.86	3.46	3.58	4.42	4.25	4.21	4.43	4.22	47.6
Avg. daily max. temp.	30.9	32.9	41.1	54.5	65.9	74.4	79.0	77.0	69.4	59.3	46.9	34.7	55.5
Avg. daily min. temp.	15.6	16.6	25.2	35.4	45.5	54.8	60.7	59.0	51.3	41.3	32.0	20.1	38.1
Clear days (avg.)*	9	8	8	7	6	6	6	8	9	10	7	8	91
Cloudy days (avg.)**	14	13	15	14	15	13	13	12	12	13	15	15	168

* Average cloud cover 30% or less
** Average cloud cover 70% or more

MASSACHUSETTS NATURAL CALENDAR

January

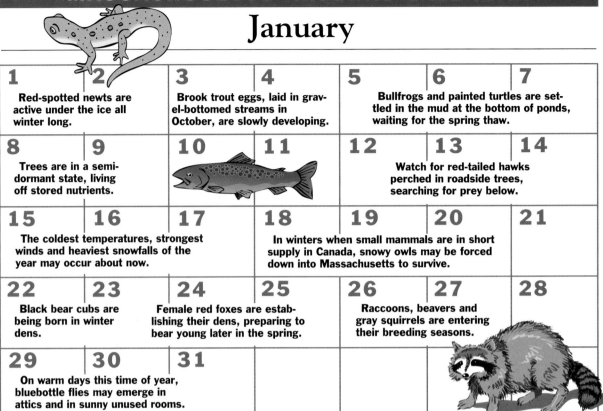

1	**2** Red-spotted newts are active under the ice all winter long.	**3** Brook trout eggs, laid in gravel-bottomed streams in October, are slowly developing.	**4**	**5** Bullfrogs and painted turtles are settled in the mud at the bottom of ponds, waiting for the spring thaw.	**6**	**7**
8	**9** Trees are in a semi-dormant state, living off stored nutrients.	**10**	**11**	**12** Watch for red-tailed hawks perched in roadside trees, searching for prey below.	**13**	**14**
15	**16** The coldest temperatures, strongest winds and heaviest snowfalls of the year may occur about now.	**17**	**18** In winters when small mammals are in short supply in Canada, snowy owls may be forced down into Massachusetts to survive.	**19**	**20**	**21**
22	**23** Black bear cubs are being born in winter dens.	**24** Female red foxes are establishing their dens, preparing to bear young later in the spring.	**25**	**26** Raccoons, beavers and gray squirrels are entering their breeding seasons.	**27**	**28**
29	**30** On warm days this time of year, bluebottle flies may emerge in attics and in sunny unused rooms.	**31**				

February

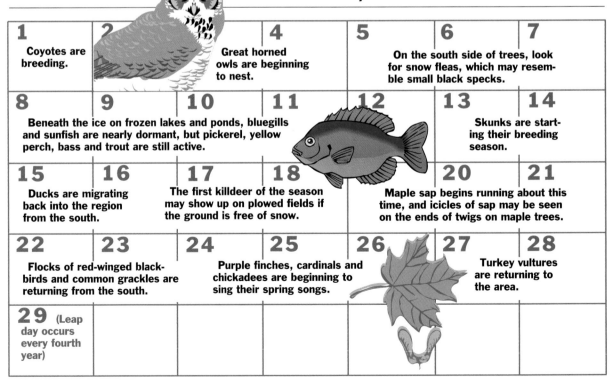

1 Coyotes are breeding.	**2**	**4** Great horned owls are beginning to nest.	**5**	**5** On the south side of trees, look for snow fleas, which may resemble small black specks.	**6**	**7**
8	**9** Beneath the ice on frozen lakes and ponds, bluegills and sunfish are nearly dormant, but pickerel, yellow perch, bass and trout are still active.	**10**	**11**	**12**	**13** Skunks are starting their breeding season.	**14**
15 Ducks are migrating back into the region from the south.	**16**	**17** The first killdeer of the season may show up on plowed fields if the ground is free of snow.	**18**	**19** Maple sap begins running about this time, and icicles of sap may be seen on the ends of twigs on maple trees.	**20**	**21**
22 Flocks of red-winged blackbirds and common grackles are returning from the south.	**23**	**24** Purple finches, cardinals and chickadees are beginning to sing their spring songs.	**25**	**26** Turkey vultures are returning to the area.	**27**	**28**
29 (Leap day occurs every fourth year)						

MASSACHUSETTS NATURAL CALENDAR

March

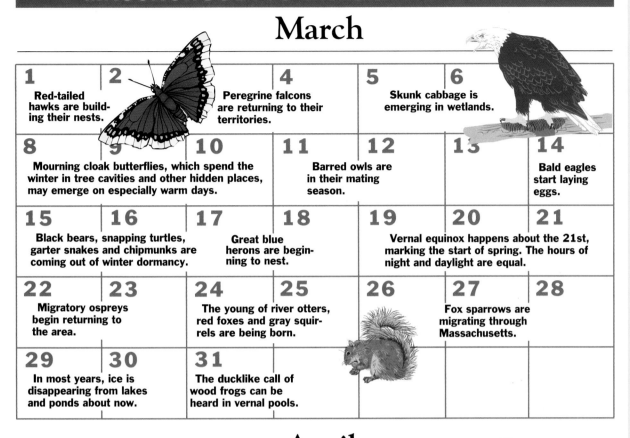

1 Red-tailed hawks are building their nests.

2

4 Peregrine falcons are returning to their territories.

5

6 Skunk cabbage is emerging in wetlands.

8 **9** **10** Mourning cloak butterflies, which spend the winter in tree cavities and other hidden places, may emerge on especially warm days.

11 **12** Barred owls are in their mating season.

13

14 Bald eagles start laying eggs.

15 **16** **17** Black bears, snapping turtles, garter snakes and chipmunks are coming out of winter dormancy.

18 Great blue herons are beginning to nest.

19 **20** **21** Vernal equinox happens about the 21st, marking the start of spring. The hours of night and daylight are equal.

22 **23** Migratory ospreys begin returning to the area.

24 **25** The young of river otters, red foxes and gray squirrels are being born.

26

27 **28** Fox sparrows are migrating through Massachusetts.

29 **30** In most years, ice is disappearing from lakes and ponds about now.

31 The ducklike call of wood frogs can be heard in vernal pools.

April

1 **2** **3** On the first warm rainy night in late March to early April, spotted and blue-spotted salamanders migrate to vernal pools to lay eggs.

4 **5** The last flurries of snow may be seen about now.

6 Bullfrogs are emerging from their winter dormancy.

8 **9** **10** Tree swallows return about this time.

11 Spring peepers can be heard calling.

12 Buds are appearing on many trees.

13 **14** Humpback whales are migrating into Massachusetts ocean waters for the summer.

15 **16** **17** Some woodland wildflowers bloom about now, before trees grow their leaves and cut off the sunlight.

18 Grass may be turning green.

19 Leaves are starting to appear on some trees.

20 **21** Shooting stars from the annual Lyrid meteor shower can be seen at night about now.

22 **23** The season's first generation of mosquitoes is starting to appear.

24 **25** Alewives are returning upriver from the ocean to spawn.

26 Dandelions are appearing on lawns, and many dogwoods are in bloom.

27 **28** Barn swallows and house wrens are returning.

29 **30** Bobcats, raccoons, coyotes and porcupines are having their young.

MASSACHUSETTS NATURAL CALENDAR

May

1	2	3	4	5	6	7
The last freezing temperatures of the spring may occur at night about now.			Marsh marigolds and wild columbines are starting to bloom.		The leaves on most trees have fully opened.	
8	**9**	**10**	**11**	**12**	**13**	**14**
Ruby-throated hummingbirds, northern orioles and gray catbirds are returning from the south.			Jack-in-the-pulpits and red trilliums are blooming.			Most warblers arrive this week.
15	**16**	**17**	**18**	**19**	**20**	**21**
Skunks and chipmunks are having their young.		Spicebush swallowtails are appearing.	American toads can be heard trilling in shallow wetlands.		Downy woodpeckers are laying their eggs.	
22	**23**	**24**	**25**	**26**	**27**	**28**
Right whale mothers and their calves are migrating out of Massachusetts waters.			White-tailed deer are having their young.		Wild lupines and blue flag irises are blooming.	
29	**30**	**31**				
Monarch butterflies are returning to the region.						

June

1	2	3	4	5	6	7
Tiger swallowtail butterflies are appearing.			June bugs are emerging, often swarming around porch lights and at screened windows at night.		Northern bluets can be seen around ponds.	
8	**9**	**10**	**11**	**12**	**13**	**14**
Black-eyed Susans, oxeye daisies and other field wildflowers are blooming.			Painted turtles are climbing out of ponds to lay their eggs.		Day lilies are blooming.	
15	**16**	**17**	**18**	**19**	**20**	**21**
The banjolike voices of green frogs can by heard at night near ponds.			Summer solstice happens about the 21st, marking the start of summer. The night will be the shortest of the year, and the number of hours of daylight will be the greatest.			
22	**23**	**24**	**25**	**26**	**27**	**28**
Fireflies can be seen at night in fields and meadows.			Bears are entering their mating season.		Young tree swallows are taking their first flights.	
29	**30**					

July

1	2	3	4	5	6	7
The flutelike trill of gray treefrogs can be heard on cloudy days.		Shorebirds that breed in Canada begin stopping in Massachusetts as they migrate south.			The season's second generation of clouded sulphur and spring azure butterflies are emerging.	
8	**9**	**10**	**11**	**12**	**13**	**14**
The whine of cicadas can be heard during the heat of the day.		Tadpoles are emerging from green frog eggs.		The greatest amount of sunshine and the least cloudiness during daylight hours occur about this time of year.		
15	**16**	**17**	**18**	**19**	**20**	**21**
Young wood frogs are leaving the water.		The young of many raptors, such as red-tailed hawks and great horned owls, are fully grown and out on their own by now.				Wild blueberries are ripening.
22	**23**	**24**	**25**	**26**	**27**	**28**
Katydids begin calling at night about this time.		Chipmunks may be having their second litter of young this year.			Jewelweed, blazing star and cardinal wildflowers are in bloom.	
29	**30**	**31**				
The hottest days of summer may occur about now and into early August.		Garter snakes may be having their young.				

August

1	2	3	4	5	6	7
Young wood ducks are taking their first flights.		Goldfinches are beginning to nest – among the latest of any of the New England songbirds to do so.			Louisiana waterthrushes begin migrating south – the earliest of any of the New England songbirds to do so.	
8	**9**	**10**	**11**	**12**	**13**	**14**
Bobcats may be having their second litter of young this year.		Leopard frogs and pickerel frogs sometimes might be seen in residential back yards.			Shooting stars from the annual Perseid meteor shower can be seen at night about now.	
15	**16**	**17**	**18**	**19**	**20**	**21**
Great blue herons are abandoning their nests for the season.		Joe-pye weed is starting to flower.			On rainy days, red-spotted newts can be seen on dirt roads in rural areas.	
22	**23**	**24**	**25**	**26**	**27**	**28**
The season's third generation of cabbage white butterflies is emerging.		The final heat wave of the summer may occur about now.			Common nighthawks are beginning to migrate in the late afternoon.	
29	**30**	**31**				
Tree swallows are moving to coastal areas, preparing to migrate.		New England asters are beginning to bloom.				

September

1	2	3	4	5	6	7
Ladybugs may gather on light-colored house trim looking for places to enter homes to spend the winter.			The eggs of wood, painted and snapping turtles are hatching.		Wild cherries and wild grapes are ripening.	

8	9	10	11	12	13	14
Monarch butterflies are starting to migrate to their winter home in Mexico.		Acorns and other nuts are ripening. Squirrels and bears are feeding heavily on them, fattening up for winter.			It's the peak of the warbler and hawk migration.	

15	16	17	18	19	20	21
Hurricane season in New England is at its height.		Goldenrod is blooming in fields and along roadsides.		In wooded areas, Jack-in-the-pulpits are producing brilliant red berries.		

22	23	24	25	26	27	28
Autumnal equinox happens about the 22nd, marking the start of fall. The hours of daylight and night will be equal.			Green darner dragonflies are migrating out of the area.		Bats are migrating – some to caves and others to southern states.	

29	30
The leaves of red maples are showing their fall colors.	

October

1	2	3	4	5	6	7
Listen for spring peepers calling in the woods on warm days.		Downy woodpeckers may drill holes in houses, trying to create a roost hole for cold winter nights.			Bullfrogs, snapping turtles and garter snakes are going into hibernation.	

8	9	10	11	12	13	14
Peregrine falcons and ospreys are migrating.		The first freezing temperatures of the fall may occur at night about now.			Fall foliage colors in Worcester County are at their peak.	

15	16	17	18	19	20	21
Robins and sparrows migrate about this time.		Fall foliage colors around Boston are at their peak.		Juncos may be arriving for the winter.	Fall foliage colors on Cape Cod and the islands are at their peak.	

22	23	24	25	26	27	28
The baby spiders of many species are emerging from eggs.		White-tailed deer are entering their breeding season.		Watch for huge evening flocks of migrating common grackles.		The last leaves of oaks may be changing color and falling.

29	30	31
Humpback whales are migrating out of Massachusetts ocean waters.		

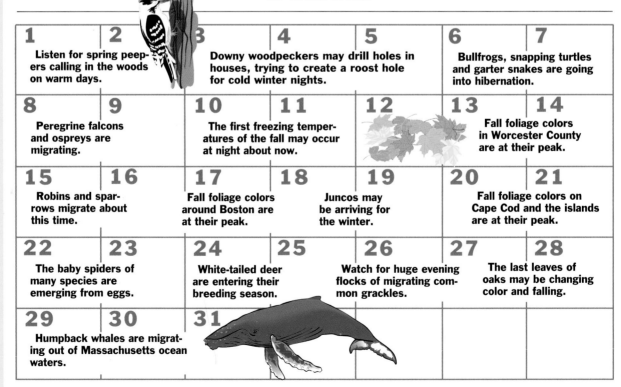

MASSACHUSETTS NATURAL CALENDAR

November

1 Flocks of cedar waxwings may be seen migrating through the region.	**2**	**3** Dandelions may still be blooming in protected areas.	**4**	**5** Crows begin to gather in nightly roosts about now and will continue to roost together until spring.	**6**	**7**
8 Check local ponds for migrating ring-necked and ruddy ducks.	**9**	**10** Eastern cottontails are out foraging for shrub twigs and buds as well as for young maples, birches and oaks.	**11**	**12**	**13** Woodchucks go into hibernation.	**14**
15 Watch for snow buntings on open fields.	**16**	**17** Shooting stars from the annual Leonid meteor shower can be seen on clear nights.	**18**	**19** The first flurries of snow may be seen about now.	**20** White wood asters and a few other fall wildflowers may still be blooming in some areas.	**21**
22 The shorebird migration is ending.	**23**	**24** Black bears are looking for a place to sleep through the winter.	**25**	**26** The first winter finches are arriving.	**27** Migrating Canada geese, flying in V formations, can be seen and heard overhead.	**28**
29 The last faint calls of meadow crickets can be heard on warm afternoons.	**30**					

December

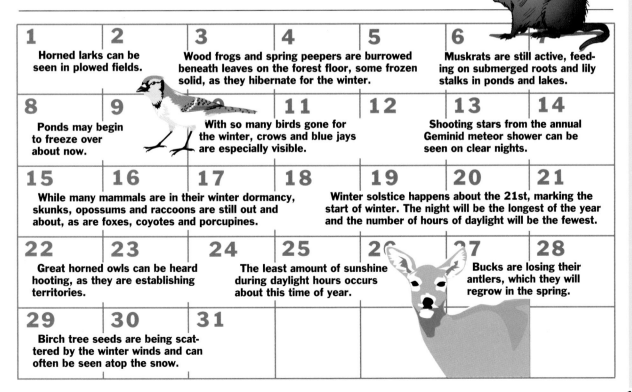

1 Horned larks can be seen in plowed fields.	**2**	**3** Wood frogs and spring peepers are burrowed beneath leaves on the forest floor, some frozen solid, as they hibernate for the winter.	**4**	**5**	**6** Muskrats are still active, feeding on submerged roots and lily stalks in ponds and lakes.	**7**
8 Ponds may begin to freeze over about now.	**9**	**10** With so many birds gone for the winter, crows and blue jays are especially visible.	**11**	**12**	**13** Shooting stars from the annual Geminid meteor shower can be seen on clear nights.	**14**
15 While many mammals are in their winter dormancy, skunks, opossums and raccoons are still out and about, as are foxes, coyotes and porcupines.	**16**	**17**	**18**	**19** Winter solstice happens about the 21st, marking the start of winter. The night will be the longest of the year and the number of hours of daylight will be the fewest.	**20**	**21**
22 Great horned owls can be heard hooting, as they are establishing territories.	**23**	**24** The least amount of sunshine during daylight hours occurs about this time of year.	**25**	**26**	**27** Bucks are losing their antlers, which they will regrow in the spring.	**28**
29 Birch tree seeds are being scattered by the winter winds and can often be seen atop the snow.	**30**	**31**				

Index

A bold number indicates a page on which a photograph of the listing appears.

Tree swallow

Osprey

Sunflower

Collecting sap to make maple syrup

Ring-billed gull

Fisher

Porcupine

Sand dunes at Plum Island, Ipswich

Round-leaved ragwort

Photo Credits

All photos are by Stan Freeman unless otherwise noted.
A photograph's position on a page is indicated as follows: T=top, C=center, B=bottom,
   R=right and L=left.

Landscapes
Paul Rezendes – 3, 69, 128
John Wawrzonek – 26, 31

General photography
Johnny Autery – 110
Les Campbell – 39BL, 41BL
Dino Diaz Jr. – 35
Gretchen Ertl – 59TR
Chris Evans – 44B
Dorothy Long (for the New England Wild
   Flower Society) – 103CL
Mark Murray – 53T
G. Francis Osborn, courtesy of Mildred
   Osborn – 33, 34, 39BR, 40BR, 41TR,
   41CR, 42TC, 42TR, 42BL, 42BC,
   43BR, 52T, 57BR, 60BR, 66BL, 71TL,
   72T, 72B, 73BR, 74B, 80T
Paul Rezendes – 80B
Pat Rowan – 106, 109
Tom Tyning – 56, 57TL, 57 upperCR, 59CR, 62CR
U.S. Fish & Wildlife Service – Tom Stehn, 5B; Dean Menhe, 42TL
Peter Yeskie – 40TL
Anonymous – 46, 47, 49, 84T, 84B

Dandelion

Gay Head cliffs, Martha's Vineyard